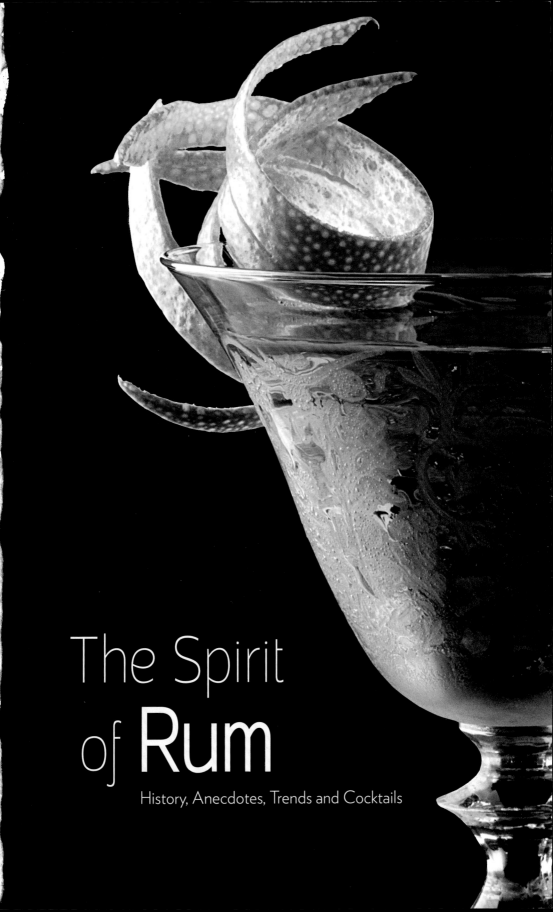

The Spirit
of Rum

History, Anecdotes, Trends and Cocktails

TEXT BY Giovanna Moldenhauer
PHOTOGRAPHS BY Fabio Petroni
COCKTAILS BY The Spirit Milano

Contents

Introduction

Rum, perhaps the only distillate to be surrounded by an aura that is both fascinating and gory, tragic and extraordinary, is currently experiencing a renaissance. The beginnings of its history in the Caribbean are closely linked with the colonial expansion of the European States. Starting in 1655 and continuing over the next three centuries, the British Royal Navy issued its sailors a rum ration. Its growing fame at the time led unscrupulous pirates and merchants to loot, pillage and trade it for their own gains, yet at the same time, enlightened personages changed the organoleptic profile, suggesting new production methods. In the late 17th century, on the small island of Marie-Galante, the missionary Père Labat contributed to making the distillate a better drink by adapting a French alembic still to produce it, while in 1830, the ex-Customs Inspector Aeneas Coffey, invented and patented the continuous still with two columns: this permitted an increase in the quantity produced and a reduction in costs, with the additional benefit of producing lighter rums.

Modern distillers can now choose which technique to use, opting for either a discontinuous or continuous still, or both, and can choose between single, double or multiple columns to produce an excellent rum, the flavor of which can be enhanced with aging in barrels.

Advertisement from the end of the 20th century, designed by Czech artist Alfons Maria Mucha, one of the most important exponents of Art Nouveau.

Today, the world of rum is extremely varied and almost boundless: to introduce you to the fascinating world of rum, we have put together over 40 labels, mostly produced by official distilleries, some of which come from countries that are emerging on the production scene, others chosen for their high symbolic value. The selection is presented according to geographical region, different production methods, niche products that are an exemplification of unusual fermentation processes and magisterial distillations. Each rum label is accompanied by a fact sheet that includes technical data, tasting notes, historical facts about the distillery, information on the selection of raw materials and on production and aging techniques.

To complete the volume, we have included 15 brand-new cocktails: inspired by the great classics, reinvented with a contemporary twist and starting from each rum's expression of its terroir. The recipes are proposed by a team of professional bartenders, who have created mixed drinks with an international flavor as an alternative to the classic way of tasting aged, complex rums at a temperature 18°C, or a perfect white rum on the rocks.

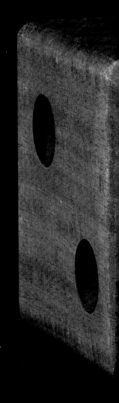

Etymology of the Word

Rum, Rhum or Ron are all the different spellings used to identify this distillate, based on the official language of the country of origin. Originally, the drink was also called *Rumbowling* or *Rumbullion*, slang words in English and French that most likely referred to the noises produced by the distillation boilers (from *rumble* and *boil* in English and *bouillir* in French). According to other theories, the name could simply come from an abbreviation of the scientific name for sugarcane, *Saccharum officinarum*. There is, however, another etymological hypothesis that traces the term back to 1655, when the Royal Navy began issuing its crews a daily distillate ration, which inevitably led to a rumble on the main deck. The allotment of rations was formalized between 1731 and 1740, first increasing and then decreasing, before eventually being watered down. The Royal Navy continued to give sailors a daily rum ration, known as the "daily tot," until 31 July 1970, when the practice was abolished, putting an end to a centuries-old association of rum and the British Navy.

By definition, rum is a beverage obtained by alcoholic fermentation and the distillation of molasses or sugarcane juice. This plant, belonging to the grass family, has been a subject of much interest for centuries, as it is the source of valuable commodities like sugar, which the Arabs, for example, believed had healing properties, and, from the 17th century, this distillate, which took its present name in around the 19th century.

To understand the exciting yet turbulent history of rum, it is necessary to start with the origin of distillation.

Rum and Its Origins

According to historical studies, the production of fermented beverages seems to have been a custom practiced by populations in ancient India and China. *The Travels of Marco Polo*, an account of his trip to Asia in the 13th century, mentions an excellent sugar wine served in the region that today corresponds to Iran. The Arabs also discovered the secrets of distillation, but the first records of the distillation of sugarcane juice date back to the 15th century, in England, first using Indian sugarcane and then that from the Americas.

The cultivation of sugarcane in the Caribbean diffused when European settlers created plantations and factories for the production of sugar. It was in the Caribbean, sometime in the first half of the 17th century, that settlers realized the

West Indies rum distillery,
1823 engraving by William Clark.

possibilities of fermenting molasses, producing a distillate that at the time was called *Rumbullion*. In Barbados, in particular, a distillation technique for producing a more alcoholic product was developed, with fewer impurities, as described in a document dated 1651: "The chief fuddling they make on the island is *Rumbullion*, alias *Kill-Divil*, and this is made of sugar canes distilled, a hot, hellish, and terrible liquor." Rum was born!

However, the work of a missionary, Père Labat, was crucial to the evolution of rum. At the end of the 17th century, he had a still sent to the island of Marie-Galante from France, more specifically from the Cognac region, which he adapted to the production of rum. Rums bearing the name of the French missionary are still produced by the oldest distillery on the Caribbean island (in this book we present a 59° version and a cocktail, Anse la Cuve, in which it is used).

Each colonizer influenced the production of rum with its native distilling traditions, improving their quality, softening

This engraving by William Clark depicts the work be carried out outside a West Indies rum distillery in the first half of the 19th century.

the taste and defining their style, which in some cases is still preserved today. While the English-speaking Guyana and other Caribbean islands mostly used discontinuous stills and then blending, the Spanish colonies specialized in long aging periods, often employing the traditional Solera system used for sherry, and the main difference in the French colonies of Martinique, Guadeloupe, Marie-Galante, Guyana and Haiti, was the use of fermented sugarcane juice rather than molasses.

Gradual fine-tuning in the production processes led to a marked improvement in taste and the possibility of a lower alcohol content, which meant that rum became a growing success in Europe and North America, resulting in increased production. Given that the Caribbean natives had almost been exterminated by diseases brought to the islands from Europe, the colonists used the slave trade to create a new workforce to cultivate the large plantations and work in the sugarcane mills: rum began playing an important role in trade between Europe and North America, the Caribbean and Africa, which also included the ignoble trade of goods, food and human beings by merchants. The distillate was initially used by plantation owners to pay their servants and slaves, as well as a pain reliever in the absence of medicine. The success of the rum trade also led to an increase in the number of attacks on sailing ships by smugglers and pirates looking for goods to loot.

Thanks to the better quality, the pleasant, captivating taste and different typologies, from the late 18th century and throughout the 19th century, rum produced in the Caribbean colonies, by several Central and South American countries, experienced a sharp increase in international demand, fueling its success and promoting its diffusion. During the 20th century, the two world wars, the Prohibition in the United

States and the Cuban revolution changed the fortunes of rum in the world. Today, rum is produced in former colonial countries like Mauritius, Madagascar and Île de la Réunion, and has conquered new horizons, such as Japan, resulting in a more extensive offering for increasingly demanding and prepared consumers.

History of sugarcane: from its origins to its diffusion and cultivation

Originally from Malaysia, sugarcane spread from South-East Asia into India about 8000 years ago. The Persians, during their expansion into India in the 6th century BC, discovered it and introduced to their territory. The soldiers of Alexander the Great, conqueror of Persia, were the first Europeans to see this plant in around 300 BC. The Greco-Roman world, however, only had a vague notion as to what it was. Herodotus and Theophrastus speak of a cane honey, made by man, different from that of bees. In 637 AD, the Arabs also discovered sugarcane, later diffusing it from Egypt to Palestine and eventually, in the 9th century, to Spain and Sicily. On colonizing Madeira in 1420, the Portuguese in turn took it to the Azores, the Canary Islands, the Cape Verde Islands and West Africa. In 1493, during his second voyage, Christopher Columbus took sugarcane to the island of Hispaniola (now the Dominican Republic). From there, European settlers introduced it into Central America and the islands of Cuba, Jamaica, Martinique and Guadeloupe, which were

A superb botanical study dating back to the late 19th century. In the top right hand corner, a section of a sugarcane stalk (Saccharum officinarum).

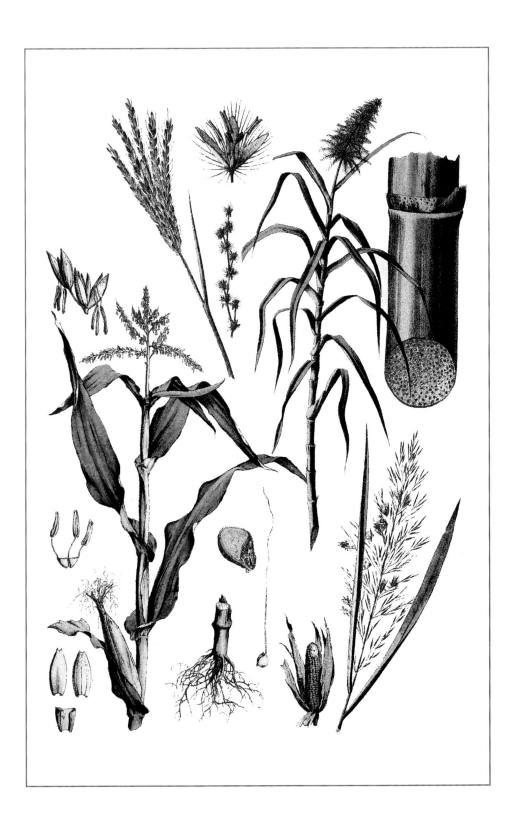

then nicknamed the "sugar islands." Sugarcane belongs to the large Gramineae family of grasses, which also includes wheat, corn and rye. The wild plant from which it originated is known as *Saccharum robustum*. The main variety cultivated nowadays is known as *Saccharum officinarum*, a hybrid developed from different sugarcane species, not only based on robustness, disease resistance, plant height and precocity, but also largely on the amount of sugar present.

New crops are created by planting sugarcane buds in areas with the most suitable climate, hot and humid between February and August, in order to ensure that each cane stalk, when fully ripe, has a high sugar content, so that the juice destined for the production of rum is of the highest quality. The type of soil in which the sugarcane is planted is not that relevant.

Sugarcane is a perennial plant, with a standard vegetative growth cycle of between 14 and 16 months, and the crops are mainly propagated by using plant cuttings. The cane stalk can reach up to 4 meters high, and the color of the stem ranges from green with yellow hues to purple. Once fully grown, the terminal bud turns into a flower, known as an "arrow." During the flowering stage, usually occurring between the twelfth and thirteenth month, the percentage of sucrose in the sugarcane increases.

Harvesting is mainly carried out by cutting the stalk at the base with a machete, as close as possible to the ground. In some areas it is still customary to burn the fields beforehand in order to scare off snakes and remove any dry leaves. Sugarcane regrows spontaneously after each harvest, although after a few years (between 4 and 7) the plants grow old and have to be replaced. To obtain quality sugarcane juice and molasses, the cane stalks must be taken to the mills for processing within 12-36 hours of cutting, so as to prevent them from drying out and losing too much juice.

There are two methods for processing sugar cane: grinding the sugar cane for the production of sugar and molasses (the term comes from the Portuguese *melaço* and it is a thick dark syrup that is a byproduct of sugar refining, which despite the high sucrose content, does not crystallize). The quality and the sugar content of the molasses are inversely related to the production of sugar.

The juice from the first grinding of the sugarcane to obtain the molasses is the best, as in the production of wine, and is defined with the technical term *Grade* A. Juice extracted with the crushing technique (*vesou* in French, *guarapo* in Spanish), on the other hand, can be sent directly to be fermented, without sugar being produced. Rhum Agricole is obtained by Vesou extraction, where the juice is first purified and then decanted, filtered and poured into the distilleries' fermentation vats.

On some Caribbean islands there are still sugarcane varieties that are not hybrids, such as the red and white varieties in Haiti, the Malanoi in Martinique, and the Rubanée and Cristalline varieties for the production of niche Rhum Agricole, given the number of bottles produced and the outstanding quality of the distillate. The increase in the production of Rhum Agricole has led to the selection of new varieties of sugarcane hybrids, created specifically for the production of the distillate, for example, the Bleue variety (blue cane), today used to produce single varietal distillates (for example, Neisson Blanc 52.50° from Martinique). The seasonal nature of sugarcane juice production is one of the reasons that led to the creation of concentrated sugar, so-called syrup or honey, which can be preserved over time but, above all, can be distilled year-round. The Barbancourt distillery, for example, makes use of it during the period when sugarcane is not harvested.

Production

Rum is obtained by fermenting sugarcane juice or molasses, by completing the following distillation process, specific to the desired product, by aging, mostly in wood, and finally by blending. Just a few steps, yet they conceal a technological and fascinating world, in which man, with his preparation, culture and ingenuity, has understood that his interpretation of each single step will change the product's final finish.

Ingredients

The ingredients needed to produce rum are sugarcane juice or molasses, yeast and water. We have already seen how sugarcane passes from the fields to being processed into juice or molasses. The yeasts are chosen according to the kind of juice or molasses that is going to be fermented, following careful analysis of the pH to assess how effective they are in converting sugars into alcohol. Water, often collected from founts or springs where it is pure, is sometimes added during the fermentation of the molasses, depending on the desired dilution level, when the sugar concentration is too high, or during the finishing process to reduce the alcohol content after distillation, as is the case for Rhum Rhum Blanc, which is diluted with rain water.

The sugar levels in molasses are not always the same: advances in extraction techniques in the sugar industry have led to a reduction in the percentage of sugar in molasses, with consequent lower alcohol content in the fermented liquid. As already mentioned, the quality of molasses is inversely proportional to the production of sugar.

Distilleries have spent much time studying the type of yeasts to use, because from the moment it is added to start the fermentation process, the process which determines the aromas and the rum itself also begins. Some distilleries choose natural or indigenous yeasts, often growing them themselves, while others indicate *Saccharomyces cerevisiae* in their product fact sheets, also used in oenology, to achieve the desired finish. Brewer's yeast is sometimes used to produce Rhum Agricole.

The production process from fermentation to distillation and aging

It is not only the choice of yeast to influence the final product sought by the distillery, but the entire production process and length of fermentation, which converts sugar into alcohol and produces carbon dioxide and heat. The duration of the production process, which takes place in open or closed tanks, is determined by the type of rum they want to obtain and can last anything from 2 to 3 days, right up to 10 or even 12. Short fermentation results in a product with a mild aroma and less aromatic compounds, while longer periods produce a liquid that contains a far greater number, making it possible to distill an extremely full-bodied rum with a distinctive flavor. Throughout the fermentation process, the distilleries control the ambient temperature to ensure that the yeasts don't cease to function too quickly and that the process is not speeded up.

Originally all rums were produced with copper discontinuous alembic stills. In the late 19th century they also began distilling with column alembic stills (continuous). To better understand the distillation process, we need to keep in mind that there are different types of alcohol, from light to heavy, and this also goes for the relative aromas. The distillation process concentrates the alcohol, separates the water, permits the Master distiller to select which congeners – aromatic components – to keep and which to discard. With a discontinuous alembic still (also known as a *pot still* and often pear-shaped) the distillation process is carried out in several stages. First, the fermented liquid is put into the still and boiled; once condensed, the vapor produces a low-alcohol liquid. During the next stage, the Master distiller can extract the so-called "heart" of the distillate, rich in alcohol, water and aromatic substances, from the tails, which evaporate at the end of the process, after eliminating the heads – toxic and with a nasty flavor – that evaporate first. How long the Master distiller takes to extract the heart depends on how many aromatic substances he or she intends to retain, as well as on how light or heavy the distillate is, the size of the boiler and the amount of alcohol present. According to Luca Gargano, owner of Velier (Italian distributor with over 20 years of experience in the world of spirits), this ancient artisan process, still used exclusively by some distilleries, makes these products Pure Single Rums, that is, an expression of the raw material and the art of the Master distiller. However, the determining reason behind the creation of column stills in the 19th century, was the need to produce greater quantities of rum following an increase in market demand. Continuous distillation, perfected and patented by Aeneas Coffey in 1830, uses a still with two columns (one for distillation and one for rectification), which are connected so that the liquid obtained by fermentation can be put in one side and come out of the other as a distillate. This system makes it possible to separate the volatile, ethyl alcohol and water fractions from the dissolved ones, like salts and organic substances, and to find specific aromatic components in the distillate. The liquid ethanol is then separated from the mixture of ethanol and water, after which the lighter heads and heavier tails are eliminated. Rums obtained with this system are light, still fairly complex, and display certain characteristics given to fermentation, which distinguish their aromatic identity. As a result of technological research and advances, alembic stills with three or multiple columns were invented, used to create rums with a precise identity under the supervision of

Master distillers. In the French West Indies, as early as the beginning of the 20th century, special single distillation columns were installed, known as "Creole", to produce Rhum Agricole. If they are small and stocky, the rum is full-bodied and low-alcohol; if they are tall, the rum is more layered and lighter. The Savalle version of the Creole column produces more aromatic, floral and complex rums. According to Luca Gargano, a distillate obtained with a Creole column is much richer, given that the aromatic complexity is much closer to a pot still rum than a product obtained from a multiple column still.

Sometimes distillers produce rum obtained from a blend of distillates made with two different distillation systems, using both a discontinuous *pot still* and a *Coffey* continuous still, which can produce either white rum that is then bottled, or wood-aged dark rum, both of which remain perfectly balanced.

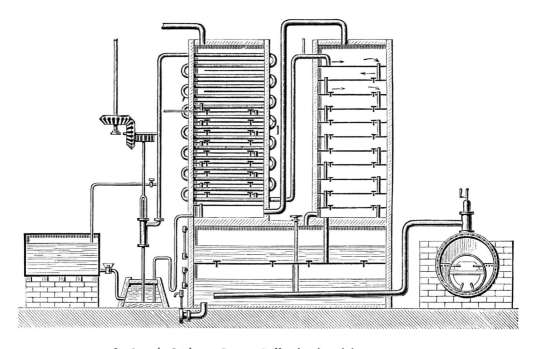

In 1830, the Irishman Aeneas Coffey developed this apparatus for continuous distillation.

At the end of the distillation process, the rum is transparent and there are aromas that cannot be easily identified. It is usually aged in oak casks that have previously held bourbon or other distillates or wines. The aging period is extremely variable, anything from a few years to more than twenty, and, depending on the quantity of heat, about 7% of the rum evaporates during this period; this loss is known as "the angels' share." Before the aging process begins, the casks are often charred inside to stimulate the distillate to interact with the air in the first few days, almost as if it is trying to capture the oxygen, which increases the aromas of vanilla, spices, chocolate, coconut and coffee. The oxidization that occurs due to the porosity of the slaves gives the distillate its color, which depends on the time spent in the cask.

The style of an aged rum depends on the type of wood chosen for the casks. The Barbancourt distillery in Haiti traditionally uses Limousin oak, whose larger pores facilitate the exchange between the rum and the oxygen, as well as creating different

The casks at the Barbancourt distillery are made from Limousin oak.
This wood, used for aging cognac, is extremely rich in tannins,
which facilitates the rum's time in the casks.

aromatic components. In countries influenced by the Spanish, the rum is often aged using the Solera system, inspired by the production of sherry. The casks are arranged in multiple tiers and only those in the top row are filled. After a year, some of the content of the casks is transferred to those in the next row down and the upper ones are filled with new rum; this process is repeated year after year until arriving at the very bottom row. When it is ready to drink, some of the rum made up of different vintages is removed from the casks in the bottom row, which are then replenished with an equal amount from the casks in the top row.

Blending and bottling

At the end of the production process, the rum in each cask has a different organoleptic profile; this is the case for both relatively young rums and aged ones. The need for distilleries to obtain a product with standard quality and content, makes the role of the Master blender decisive: to create the desired rum, he or she must combine different vintages, from different casks and with different alcohol contents. If different vintages are mixed, countries such as Barbados, Jamaica, the Antilles and French Guiana have laws that require that the youngest vintage is written on the label. For aged rums made with the Solera system, the average vintage is indicated, while for others the label displays the oldest. A rum obtained from a mixture of different vintages, with different periods of aging, is defined as blended, while if it is obtained from a mixture of rums that have been aged for the same length of time, it is defined as vintage.

After the final blend has been assembled, the alcohol content is reduced by adding demineralized water, to arrive at the alcohol percentage required to be put on the market. To keep the rum in the bottle clear, the ethanol-water mixture is cooled (below zero) and then filtered prior to bottling.

Around the World in 41 Rums

A selection of rums

The choices that led us to select 41 different types of rum, were based firstly on geographical criteria and therefore on the production methods that permit the Master distillers and blenders to turn the raw materials, in many cases indigenous, into high-quality products. In this journey through the world of rum, we will learn about Caribbean Rhum Agricole, rums from the Americas and a few products from exotic southern hemisphere and Asian countries. Most of the labels are produced by official distilleries, guaranteeing their quality.

Guadeloupe, Haiti, Marie-Galante and Martinique, French colonies since the 18th century, produced sugar obtained from sugarcane, which was one of the goods they supplied to their motherland. When, in the 19th century, Napoleon Bonaparte decided to encourage the cultivation of European sugar beet to guarantee France's sugar supply, the cultivation of sugarcane in the Caribbean began to decline, with a consequent decrease in the amount of molasses available to distilleries. This led rum producers at the time to use freshly squeezed sugarcane juice and consequently to develop Rhum Agricole. Over time, the production processes have evolved, but the raw material has remained the same, and for this reason, the term Rhum Agricole can only be used if accompanied by a Designation of Origin on the label.

Rums from the Americas have characteristics specific to their territory of origin. In Barbados, where they have been practicing the technique of distillation since the 18th century, they use both discontinuous and column alembic stills, while the style of Bermudan rum was created by the Gosling family in the second half of the 19th century. In Colombia, they create blends from rum that has been aged with the Solera system for 12 years, a production method that is also by the only distillery in El Salvador to produce molasses-based rums. In Costa Rica, they produce rums that have been aged for long periods of time (over 10 years). The art of *Ron Ligero* has been handed down from generation to generation in Cuba, while rums produced in Guatemala are medium-bodied and lend themselves particularly well to aging at high altitudes. Molasses is the raw material used in Guyana, obtained from Demerara cane sugar. Haiti, once the largest producer of sugar and rum in the Caribbean, today has over 500 artisan and clandestine distilleries, which at times produce limited quantities. Jamaica, which has an official rum classification system, produces overproof distillates with specific fermentation and distillation techniques. In Mexico, rum production is based on ancient traditions while using modern equipment. In recent years, there has been a growing appreciation of distillates produced in Nicaragua, obtained by aging different vintages. In Panama, there are numerous examples of excellent aged rum, while in Peru they use an ancient recipe that is produced with the Solera system. Puerto Rican rums, which must adhere to a production specification, focus greatly on the raw material, style and respect for regulations. In the Dominican Republic, the *Maestros Roneros* (Master rum makers) give the distillate, often aged, a precise identity with their choice of casks and aging methods. The small local distillery in Saint Lucia uses casks that first contained high quality bourbon, while in Trinidad & Tobago, the rums are produced by distillation in a column alembic still, followed by aging in wood casks. Venezuela, on the other hand, is famous for dark amber rums, aged in oak casks.

More exotic, yet equally as interesting, is a rum produced in the Land of the Rising Sun, an excellent example of the Japanese's skills in the art of fermentation, and another made on Reunion Island, produced with long and unusual fermentation processes. Madagascan rums display hints of vanilla, one of the island's typical plants, while in Mauritius, distillates are made with pure sugarcane juice and have very different styles.

In the past, rums were often recognized for their French, English or Spanish style, each very different due to the raw material and production processes used. Today, the vast and variegated world of rum is much more intricate, complex and fascinating, as this short journey through the selected labels intends to demonstrate.

Caribbean Rhum Agricole

Damoiseau Blanc 40°

Domaine de Séverin XO

Reimoneng Cuvée Spéciale Blanc Centenaire

Barbancourt Réserve Spéciale 8 Ans

Clairin Casimir 3.1

Bielle Vieux 2009

Père Labat 59

Rhum Rhum Blanc PMG

Neisson Blanc

Saint James Vieux

Trois Rivières Cuvée de l'Océan

In this section, we present a selection of Rhum Agricole from the Caribbean. There are three different expressions of rum from Guadeloupe: the leader distillery Damoiseau produces a white rum with 40° alcohol by volume; Domaine de Séverin, an historical family of producers, offer an XO version that is aged for six years; Reimonenq Blanc proposes a special version, produced to celebrate the distillery's one hundredth anniversary.

From Haiti, there are two unusual expressions: Clairin, considered the last natural rum in the Caribbean, obtained from organically grown sugarcane and by discontinuous distillation, the result of which is a surprisingly aromatic product; Barbancourt, which still ages the distillate according to a recipe created in 1862 by its founder, originally from Charente. On Marie-Galante, a small island not far from Guadeloupe, we can find: Bielle, a 2009 vintage Rhum Agricole, one of the most authentic in the world; Père Labat, produced by the oldest distillery on the island, which offers a 59° version produced in limited numbers; Rhum Rhum, obtained with specific alembic stills designed by Master distiller Gianni Vittorio Capovilla, a distillate that tantalizes the taste buds from start to finish. Finally, we propose three very different rums from Martinique: Neisson, produced with an unusual cultivar of blue sugarcane from the north of the island and with an alcoholic strength of 52.50°; Saint James, obtained by double distillation and aged in Durmast oak casks for 3 to 6 years; Trois Rivières, made with sugarcane grown near the ocean in the extreme south of Martinique, using a column still. Whatever the production method, all types of Rhum Agricole have an interesting, richer olfactory profile, because the aromatic substances remain unaltered.

Damoiseau Blanc 40°

Country: *Guadeloupe (France)*
Producer: *Hervé Damoiseau*
ABV: *40%*
Bottle: *70 cl*

Typology: *Rhum Agricole*
Production: *continuous distillation in a single column still, 3 to 6 months aging in Durmast oak casks formerly used for bourbon.*

The Damoiseau family, owners of the Bellevue distillery in Guadeloupe, just outside Le Moule on the island of Grande Terre, have been producing a high quality Rhum Agricole since 1942, respecting the Appellation of Origin and tradition of the French Antilles. Leader of agricultural rums in Guadeloupe, Damoiseau distributes over 2 million liters, of which 75% is in Guadeloupe and the Caribbean, with significant success in both these and the French market, where Damoiseau is the most consumed Rhum Agricole. Upon arrival, the distillery checks the state, freshness and weight of the sugarcane, verifying the pH in view of producing a quality product and correct, fair payment to suppliers. The rums in the range are made exclusively with sugarcane juice, which after having been carefully squeezed, is fermented at a temperature of 35°C for between 24 to 36 hours, with the addition of *Saccharomyces cerevisiae* yeast. After distillation, the Rhum Blanc, with an alcohol content of about 70%, is stored with its full alcohol strength for between 3 and 6 months, in wood casks with a capacity between 10,000 and 60,000 liters. During this maturation period, the volatile components evaporate with aeration and mixing. Before bottling, the last stage of the production process, the rum is reduced to 40° with the addition of water.

Tasting

Color: *crystalline and clear.*
Nose: *opens with delicate sweet notes marked by sugarcane, then becoming floral and slightly spicy.*
Palate: *dry, balanced, strong flavor with exotic notes.*
Finish: *delicate and persistent.*
Ideal: *on the rocks.*

Domaine de Séverin XO

Country: *Guadeloupe (France)*
Producer: *Marsolle family*
ABV: *45%*
Bottle: *70 cl*

Typology: *Rhum Vieux Agricole*
Production: *continuous distillation in a single column still, 6 years aging in casks formerly used for bourbon, followed by blending.*

The Séverin distillery, founded in 1928 by Henri Marsolle, is immersed in the lush greenery of Guadeloupe, in Sainte Rose, in the French Antilles. The ancestors of the Marsolle family arrived in Guadeloupe with the first French settlers in around 1635, and they started producing rum in 1893. Since then, at Domaine de Séverin stories and experiences from the past have been handed down from father to son. The paddle wheel is a symbol of these ancient traditions. Purchased in 1933 to replace the old one from the 18th century, the distillery – the last in the French Antilles – used it to produce energy from the river that flows close to the factory, to process the sugarcane, before being replaced by alternative energy sources in 2010. Séverin, a family-run distillery still owned by the original family, produces one of the best white rums, one of the most authentic in the area, which they bottle themselves.

Tasting

Color: *light amber, crystalline.*
Nose: *elegant hints of vanilla and banana which evolve slowly in the glass.*
Palate: *smooth, powerful attack with a dominant roasted note, followed by notes of vanilla and sugar.*
Finish: *round, leaving the palate dry and slightly spicy.*
Ideal: *straight up.*

Reimoneng
Cuvée
Spéciale
Blanc
Centenaire

Country: *Guadeloupe (France)*
Producer: *Reimonenq family*
ABV: *50%*
Bottle: *70 cl*

Typology: *Rhum Blanc Agricole*
Production: *made from pure sugarcane juice, column distilled and left to rest in steel tanks for 15 months.*

The Reimonenq distillery, founded on the island of Guadeloupe in the French Antilles in 1916, soon specialized in the sole production of agricultural rums, obtained by the distillation of pure sugarcane juice. Today, more than a century after its establishment, Leopold Reimonenq and his family continue the artisan tradition of distillation, facilitated by modern equipment. The property's twenty hectares of sugarcane crops, together with other local crops, guarantee the smallest distillery in the French colonies an annual production of 300,000 liters of rum. The sugarcane is harvested, cut and ground by electric mills; the juice is left to ferment in tanks that are open to the air for between 24 and 48 hours, after which it is distilled in a special column alembic still that is heated by means of an electrical heat exchanger rather than direct heat: this avoids the unpleasant odors of distillation heads, permits more accurate control over the alcohol content and focuses on the heart of the distillation, the "cœur de chauffe" in French. The white rum leaves the distillation column at 60°/70° and is of the finest quality; it is then left to rest in steel tanks before being aged in wood casks of various sizes. During the long maturation processes, the rum is stirred to obtain a decidedly rich aromatic profile. At the same time, during the 15 months the alcohol content decreases and the rum becomes smoother. This rum was produced to celebrate the one hundredth anniversary of the distillery, which also houses a museum dedicated to rum.

Tasting
Color: *clear and limpid.*
Nose: *fresh, fragrant, opening with notes of lime and sugarcane, leading to floral notes and ending with grassy notes, fragrances of myrtle and juniper.*
Palate: *its powerful character bursts on the palate, with notes of walnut, offering a rich, yet unaggressive flavor.*
Finish: *dry with sweet notes.*
Ideal: *on the rocks or in a Leopold Heritage cocktail.*

Barbancourt
Réserve
Spéciale
8 Ans

Country: *Haiti*
Producer: *Thierry Gardère and sons*
ABV: *43%*
Bottle: *70 cl*

Typology: *Rhum Agricole Réserve*
Production: *double distillation in discontinuous copper alembic stills, aged in Limousin white oak casks, formerly used for cognac, for 8 years.*

In 1862, Dupré Barbancourt, originally from the French region of Charente, the area where cognac is produced, perfected the recipe for the rum that bears his name. He used the Charentais method of double distillation in discontinuous copper alembic stills, at the time used only for the very best cognacs, with the aim of obtaining a unique product. Rhum Barbancourt immediately received countless awards and accolades throughout the world. It is the largest distillery in Haiti, still owned by the same family, and has been managed lately by Thierry Gardère and then by his sons, fourth and fifth generation of the family. The distillery has 120 hectares of sugarcane crops that are dedicated to the production of Barbancourt rum, with more than 400 agricultural workers. The hand-harvested sugarcane is pressed four times to obtain the sugarcane juice, which is then mixed with a formula of special yeast and left to ferment for 36 to 48 hours. Asides from the skillful mastery behind its distillation, what makes this rum so unique is that it is aged exclusively in French white oak casks (unlike other rums produced on the island). This type of wood has larger pores than other varieties, facilitating an optimal exchange between the distillate and the oxygen in the air. This rum bears Special Reserve and 5 stars on its label, merit of the unique details incorporated into the production process. It enhances any drink to which it is added. The dry character and light structure of the Réserve Spéciale pair perfectly with the Caribbean island's hot and spicy food.

Tasting
Color: *bright golden.*
Nose: *elegant and complex with notes of honey, green apple, apricot, ginger and hints of Sauternes.*
Palate: *smooth, silky, maintaining its complexity, with hints of apricot jam and orange marmalade, barley sugar, nougat, sugarcane juice, ginger.*
Finish: *persistent with lingering notes of ginger and honey.*
Ideal: *straight up or on the rocks.*

Clairin
Casimir
3.1

CLAIRIN CASIMIR
RHUM PUR JUS DE CANNE
53,4% vol. Distillerie Faubert Casimir
Barraderes - Haiti   70 cl ℮

Country: *Haiti*

Producer: *The Spirit of Haiti*

ABV: *53.40%*

Bottle: *70 cl*

Typology: *Pure Single Rhum Agricole*

Production: *discontinuous distillation, bottled with the same alcohol by volume as it has when it comes out of the still.*

Faubert Casimir carries on the work started in Barradères by his father Duncan, in 1979, where he organically cultivates 50 hectares of tender Hawaii White and Hawaii Red sugarcane, without the use of synthetic chemicals like herbicides, fertilizers or fungicides. Once harvested, carried out strictly by hand and only when the cane is fully ripe, the sugarcane is transported to from the fields to The Spirit of Haiti distillery in Saint Michel de l'Attalaye on animal-drawn carts. After having obtained the pure sugarcane juice, it undergoes spontaneous fermentation for at least 120 hours. During this process, Faubert adds citronella leaves, cinnamon and, for certain cuvées, ginger; this is what makes Clairin rums Haiti's rums par excellence. The discontinuous distillation takes place inside alembic stills with a maximum of 5 copper plates in direct contact with the flame; a technique that can be defined as archaic. The product is then bottled, with the same alcohol content it has when it comes out of the still and without being filtered. The rums produced by the distillery – Casimir, Vaval and Sajous – are made with different varieties of sugarcane, using different fermentation and distillation processes, production techniques and aromaticity, but, above all, they stand out from all the other rums produced in Haiti, where there are 532 distilleries, some of which are tiny, thanks to the artistic and artisan production methods.

Tasting

Color: *colorless and crystalline.*

Nose: *opens with notes of ginger and cinnamon, followed by sugarcane juice, very ripe William pears and subtle hints of black pepper.*
It evolves into a fusion of licorice, nutmeg and cloves, lemon and lemongrass.
It is extremely complex from start to finish.

Palate: *delicate. Opens with notes of peach, pear, intoxicating flowers, spices, leading to a grassy finish followed by sensations of sugarcane, ivy, rose.*

Finish: *long. The taste of tiger balm prolongs the spicy and therapeutic character of the finish, leading to vegetal hints of sugarcane and grassy hints of lichen, ivy.*
The aftertaste fades into hints of rose, raspberry, apricot jellies and jams. Aromas of spicy ginger, cinnamon, walnut oil and almond linger in the empty glass.

Ideal: *straight up or in a Baron Samedi cocktail.*

Bielle Vieux 2009

Country: *Marie-Galante (France)*
Producer: *Bielle*
ABV: *42%*
Bottle: *50 cl*

Typology: *Rhum Vieux Agricole*
Production: *distillation in an ancient three column Savalle alembic still and aged in wood casks formerly used for cognac. Unfiltered.*

The Bielle distillery was established by Jean-Pierre Bielle in the heart of the small Caribbean island of Marie-Galante in 1769, on a plateau at an altitude of 110 meters. In the 1980s, Dominique Thierry reunited the family heirs and rebuilt the distillery, deciding to keep the remains of the old sugar refinery as a historical memento and creating an open-air museum which preserves the instruments once used to produce sugar. The ancient varieties of sugarcane used to produce the rums come from 50 hectares on the property and from over 100 small local farmers; the cane is still transported carts drawn by oxen. Today the distillery, firmly established as the island's undisputed leader producer in the last decade, produces Rhum Agricole according to ancient artisan techniques, remaining a fine example of a tradition that has been handed down from generation to generation. Another of Bielle's distinguishing characteristics is the fact that it does not burn the fields after the sugarcane has been harvested. By avoiding this widespread practice, dictated by the need to eliminate snakes and weeds, Bielle rums do not display any burnt notes.

Tasting

Color: *golden yellow with dark amber highlights.*
Nose: *the fragrances range from sweet, ripe yellow fruit to spices, cinnamon in particular. The underlying notes of wood are evident and enrich the bouquet.*
Palate: *delivers a dry flavor, with a wonderfully warm, rich, round and full body.*
Ideal: *straight up.*

RHUM BLANC
AGRICOLE

PÈRE
LABAT
59

ISLE DE ... GALANTE

70 cl.   59% vol.

Père Labat 59

Country: *Marie-Galante (France)*
Producer: *Distillerie Poisson*
ABV: *59%*
Bottle: *70 cl*

Typology: *Rhum Agricole*
Production: *continuous distillation in single column still.*

This Rhum Agricole bears the mark of an historic brand, whose name derives directly from Jean-Baptiste Labat, better known as Père Labat. When the French missionary arrived in Martinique, he continued the study on distillation started by Father Du Tertre. He then put his research into practice, having a cognac still sent from France, which he modified to produce rum. The result was the Labat alembic still, the very first to begin distilling in the French Antilles at the end of the 17th century. The small Poisson distillery, the oldest on the island of Marie-Galante, situated in Grand Bourg, produces Père Labat rum, an extremely aromatic artisan product of great quality, elegance and finesse. The distillery still preserves the old alembic stills, which over time have been joined by more modern distillation systems. This Rhum Agricole 59 is made from pure sugarcane juice distilled in a column still, and is produced in limited numbers.

Tasting

Color: *clear and crystalline.*
Nose: *the olfactory profile displays delicate aromas with dominant fruity notes and fresh vegetal hints.*
Palate: *smooth, sophisticated flavor which despite the high alcohol content delicately reveals elegant aromatic notes.*
Finish: *great persistence.*
Ideal: *straight up or in an Anse la Cuve cocktail.*

Rhum Rhum Blanc PMG

Country: *Marie-Galante (France)*
Producer: *Rhum Rhum*
ABV: *56%*
Bottle: *70 cl*
Typology: *Pure Single Rhum Agricole*

Production: *double distillation in bain-marie alembic stills, designed by Master distiller Gianni Vittorio Capovilla and manufactured in Germany at the Müller workshop; reduced to 56% alcohol by volume.*

Rhum Rhum is produced in the Bielle distillery on the island of Marie-Galante, using specific stills designed by Capovilla and made in Germany by the artisan Müller. The introduction of these stills, with a capacity of 300 and 1200 liters, between 2005 and 2007, permitted the distillery to create two different types of Pure Single Rhum, including a 41° version. Rhum Rhum is obtained from a rare, naturally cultivated red sugarcane, which is cut with a traditional "coutelas" and taken to the distillery on oxen-drawn carts. During the production process, the fresh brown sugarcane juice is not diluted with water and no chemicals or acidifying agents are added. After being left to ferment in thermo-regulated stainless steel tanks for 5/6 days, the juice undergoes double distillation, after which the alcohol content is reduced to 56% with pure rain water. Before bottling, Rhum Rhum Blanc PMG is stabilized in stainless steel for about one year.

Tasting

Color: *colorless.*
Nose: *opens with fruity notes of peach, pear, liquor-soaked cherry and raspberry, pineapple, passion fruit, leading to notes of leather, tobacco, varnish, freshly-cut grass and fresh ginger.*
Palate: *rich, generous, with fruity and almondy notes, followed by spices like star anise, clove and cinnamon, evolving into notes of grapefruit, bergamot, lilac and lily of the valley. Finally, notes of vanilla, pistachio and almond.*
Finish: *long, clean. Fruity returns, in part of candied fruit, but also jammy notes of cherry and strawberry. The fragrances of geranium and rose petals encompass mineral notes of pencil lead with their fragrance, leaving a lingering sensation of star anise.*
Ideal: *on the rocks.*

Neisson Blanc

Country: *Martinique (France)*
Producer: *Neisson*
ABV: *52.50%*
Bottle: *70 cl*

Typology: *Rhum Agricole*
Production: *continuous distillation in copper Savalle column still.*

Neisson is a small distillery just outside the fishing village of La Carbet, founded in 1931 and today run by Grégory Neisson Vernant, third generation of the family, who is the last Master distiller owner on the island. Only sugarcane from the plantations on the 40-hectare property is used; the crops grow in the volcanic soils surrounding the distillery, close to the sea, where the climatic conditions are ideal for the plants to fully ripen. Neisson continues to cultivate three varieties of autochthonous sugarcane: Malanoi, Rubanée and Cristalline, which, after a long battle, have now been included in the product specification for the Martinique Rhum Agricole AOC. The slow fermentation of the pure blue sugarcane juice and its continuous distillation in a single column still lasts up to 72 hours, the longest period for any rum in the French Antilles, thereby developing a unique aromatic complexity. Grégory is currently experimenting with the production of selected native yeasts on his property. The distillation of Blanc 52.50°, carried out in a 1938 copper Savalle column still at a temperature of 73° by the Master distiller himself, is artisan, meticulous, almost maniacal, with a low alcohol content, in the spirit of producing a rum with great structure. The tasting version is only made with Bleue sugarcane, cultivated in Thieubert's plots around the distillery. Neisson produces two other classic versions of Blanc, 50° and 55°, as well as L'Esprit Bio, a new white rum bottled with the same alcohol content it has when it comes out of the still, specially blended to produce 70% alcohol by volume; this rum has been produced since 2016, when a few hectares of the property were converted to organic land. When left to rest 6 months in stainless steel vats, the alcohol content remains unaltered.

Tasting
Color: *clear and crystalline.*
Nose: *intense with typical aromas of sugarcane, citrus fruit, banana, with an ethereal note of solvent and a slight hint of aniseed.*
Palate: *ample with a honey and citrus fruit flavor.*
Finish: *intense, round and aromatic with licorice returns.*
Ideal: *on the rocks.*

Saint James Vieux

Country: *Martinique (France)*
Producer: *Saint James*
ABV: *42%*
Bottle: *70 cl*
Typology: *Rhum Vieux Agricole*

Production: *Charentais double distillation method in discontinuous alembic stills, aged in small Durmast oak casks for between three and six years.*

In 1882, Paulin Lambert, an enterprising Marseillaise merchant of Jamaican rum, created Plantations Saint James, registering the name and design of the famous square bottle that still identifies this brand today. In the same period, he bought four distilleries, where he started to produce rum, and he was one of the first entrepreneurs to use advertising to sell an alcoholic product in a bottle. He became a leader producer in Martinique and France, exporting to various world markets. In 1967, Saint James was bought by the Picon consortium, which in turn sold the company to Cointreau in 1971; in 2003 it became part of the La Martiniquaise group. The last forty years of Saint James's history have been marked by the presence of Jean-Claude Benoit, the company's General Manager and probably the most important man in the world of Rhum Agricole for his string of achievements that continues today. The Saint James range of products is the most extensive and complete in Martinique and the entire Caribbean. This particular rum is part of the traditional line, which includes, among others, 7, 12 and 15-year-old rums and three Hors d'Age vintage rums.

Tasting

Color: *very intense coppery yellow with amber highlights.*
Nose: *smell of orange marmalade and cinnamon,*
together with sweet hints of vanilla and butter, notes of dry biscuits and aniseed.
Palate: *smooth, round flavor, yet with a decisive embracing taste of alcohol that*
brings out the numerous fruity returns.
Finish: *clean with lingering persistence of cloves and nutmeg.*
Ideal: *straight up.*

Trois
Rivières
Cuvée de
l'Océan

Country: *Martinique (France)*
Producer: *B. B. S.*
ABV: *42%*
Bottle: *70 cl*
Typology: *Rhum Agricole*

Production: *pure sugarcane juice distilled in a copper column still, maturation in Durmast oak barrels of different origins.*

The Trois Rivières company was founded in 1660 by Nicolas Fouquet, Superintendent of Finance under Louis XIV, who awarded himself 2000 hectares of land in the south of Martinique. However, it was only 110 years later, after various changes in ownership, that the company started cultivating sugarcane, opening three sugar refineries, some evidence of which can still be found today. In 1785, the land was bought by Etienne Isaïe Marraud Des Grottes, which started producing rum as well as sugar. In 1905, Amédée Aubéry bought Trois Rivières, modernizing it and deciding to produce just rum. His son enlarged the plantation, moved the distillery and focused production on Rhum Agricole. In 1953, the Marraud Des Grottes family, who owned the Duquesne brand, bought back the property and sold Trois Rivières aged rums under the Duquesne trademark until 1972. Over the following years, the diffusion of Martinique rums at international level led to the expansion of the distillery and the introduction of a second distillation column. In 1994, the B. B. S. company, already owner of La Mauny rum, took over the distillery that two years later was able to boast the production of rums with the Martinique AOC (Appellation d'Origine Contrôlée). The production of Cuvée de l'Océan begins in February, when the sugarcane, coming from Anse Trabaud in the far south of Martinique, is selected on the basis of sugar content and cut. The sugarcane juice, extracted by pressing and crushing, is filtered and put into fermentation tanks where the action of yeasts transforms it in 24 hours, after which it is distilled in a copper column still. The rum is then matured in Durmast oak casks, where the process is accelerated by the tropical climate, before being selected by the Master distiller Daniel Baudin. This rum does not undergo chill filtering.

Tasting
Color: *coloress and crystalline.*
Nose: *characterized by seductive scents of sugarane flowers and displaying original mineral notes of salt and iodine.*
Palate: *a powerful rum, rich, thick and displaying great minerality. The ocean, from which it takes is name, is nearby, and the flavors acquired from the sea combine perfectly with the vegetal notes of sugarcane.*
Finish: *long and expressive, evolving into mineral and salty notes.*
Ideal: *straight up or in a Papillon cocktail.*

Rums from the Americas

Doorly's XO
Mount Gay Black Barrel
Plantation 20th Anniversary
Gosling's Black Seal 80 Proof
La Hechicera Fine Aged Rum
Centenario Gran Legado 12 Años
Santiago de Cuba Carta Blanca
Cihuatán Solera 12 Reserva Especial
Hampden Fire Velvet Overproof
Worthy Park Rum-Bar White Overproof
Botran Reserva Blanca
El Dorado 8 Years Old
Sol Tarasco Extra Aged Charanda
Flor de Caña Gran Reserva 7 Years Old
Ron Abuelo 7 Años
Malteco Reserva del Fundador 20 Años
Zafra Master Reserve 21 Años
Ron Millonario Reserva Especial 15 Años
Don Q Añejo
Brugal Extra Viejo
Presidente Marti 15 Años Solera
Admiral Rodney St. Lucia Rum
Angostura 1919
Diplomático Reserva Exclusiva
Roble Viejo Extra Añejo

In Central and part of South America, sugarcane, in all its varieties, is a quality raw material that is mostly interpreted using centenary traditions. There are three very different rums from Barbados: Doorly's XO is a 6 to 12-year double maturation blend; Mount Gay Black Barrel is aged in a special selection of casks; Plantation 20th Anniversary is produced by two different types of distillation. Bermuda offers Gosling's, a rum with an unusal style. La Hechicera, from Colombia, is distilled using the Solera system and aged between 12 and 21 years. In Costa Rica, Centenario Gran Legado 12 Años is made from sugarcane juice. The Cuban Santiago de Cuba Carta Blanca is a *Ron ligero*, an expression of tradition. El Salvador offers the 12-year Cihuatán, distilled using the Solera system, while we present 2 overproof rums from Jamaica: Hampden Fire Velvet, made by triple distillation, and Worthy Park Rum-Bar, produced by the oldest working distillery in the world. Guatemala is represented by Botran Reserva Blanca, made with sugarcane juice concentrate. El Dorado 8 Years Old from Guyana is made with Demerara molasses. Mexico proposes Sol Tarasco, an ancestral aged rum known as "Charanda", while in Nicaragua we find Flor de Caña Gran Reserva 7 years old, a rum with a multi-faceted tasting profile. Panama is represented by three different expressions: Abuelo 7 Años, made with molasses in a multiple column still; the Guatemalan-style Malteco 20 Años, made with sugarcane juice concentrate; Zafra Master Reserve 21 Años, a limited edition. The Peruvian Ron Millonario 15 Años is distilled in three stages. Don Q Añejo, a Puerto Rican rum, is made in accordance with the product specification. The Dominican Republic is represented by Brugal Extra Viejo made with molasses and aged for 8 years, and Presidente Marti 15 Años Solera, obtained from sugarcane juice and syrup. Saint Lucia proposes Admiral Rodney, a 12-year rum with an unusual choice of casks. In Trinidad & Tobago we find Angostura 1919, a rum blend aged for a minimum of 8 years. The selection ends in Venezuela, with Diplomático Reserva Exclusiva, a blend of 60 different rums and Roble from the heart of the distillate, aged 8 years.

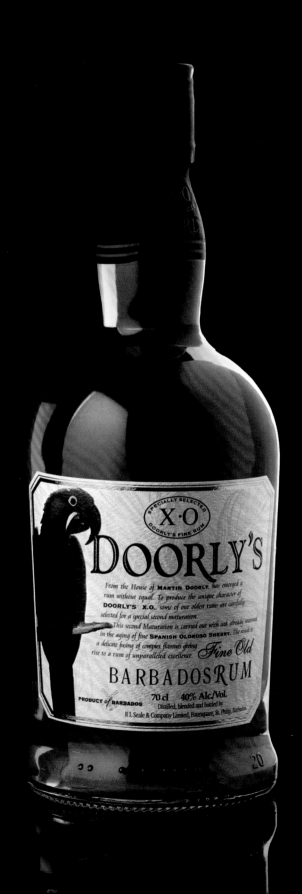

Doorly's XO

Country: *Barbados*
Producer: *Foursquare Distillery*
ABV: *40%*
Bottle: *70 cl*
Typology: *Blended Rum*

Production: *continuous and discontinuous distillation, respectively in a Coffey still and a pot still, aged in wood casks, assembly of rums ranging from 6 to 12 years, followed by maturation in casks formerly used for Oloroso sherry.*

In 1916, the government of the British colony of Barbados approved the Rum Duty Act, which had a great influence on making the Rum industry what it is today. The new law required that a license be issued for distillation and that new distilleries could only sell rum in a cask, not bottled. Therefore, many traders in Bridgetown became bottlers, including Martin Doorly, whose Doorly's Macaw Rum became the first rum made in Barbados to be exported. Doorly's is the main line of rums produced by the Foursquare Distillery in St. Philip. Richard Seale is considered one of the best rum distillers in the Caribbean, and his distillery is one of the most modern, technological and eco-sustainable in Barbados. It was also designed to be energy efficient and has the most advanced recycling and waste disposal systems on the island. Doorly's XO and the other rums in the range are obtained by vacuum distillation, reducing the temperature required for boiling and thereby avoiding unnatural aromas in the rum. The final assembly is composed of 6 to 12-year rums which are aged a second time in Spanish Oloroso sherry casks, producing a complex, creamy and velvety rum. Like the 3, 5 and 12-year rums, XO rums are made with molasses, do not contain sugars and are distilled and bottled in Barbados.

Tasting

Color: *intense, bright amber.*
Nose: *characteristic and intriguing bouquet of fruit, spices, Sichuan pepper, orange, dry and toasted fruit.*
Palate: *creamy and velvety with dominant notes of sugarcane and hazelnut.*
Finish: *harmonious, elegant, long.*
Ideal: *straight up, on the rocks or with a Davidoff Nicaragua Toro cigar.*

Mount Gay Black Barrel

Country: *Barbados*
Producer: *Mount Gay*
ABV: *43%*
Bottle: *70 cl*
Typology: *Handcrafted Rum*

Production: *double distillation in a single column copper alembic still, double maturation, first in toasted Durmast oak casks and then, for the finish, in very charred Durmast oak casks formerly used for bourbon.*

The year in which the distillery was founded, 1703, as still proudly displayed on the bottles today, makes Mount Gay one of the oldest labels in the Caribbean. It was founded by Sir John Gay, a respected businessman in Barbados, who chose to open the distillery in St. Michael based on the suggestion of his friend John Sorber, an expert on distillation. St. Michael is located on the south coast of the island and at the time was known as Mount Gilboa. Over the years, the distillation process at Mount Gay has been redefined, and today the company boasts over 310 years of tradition, artisanality and expertise. Black Barrel, the latest creation of Master Blender Allen Smith, is a small batch; an artisan blend of matured and aged rum. It is made with a selection of the best sugarcane molasses, obtained from plants harvested from the plantations nearby. The molasses is sterilized and fermented, usually from 22 to 48 hours and together with quality yeasts, followed by double distillation in single column copper alembic stills. At the end of the process, the rum has an alcoholic content of 95% and, before being put in casks for aging, it is decreased to 68% with pure spring water from Barbados. For the finishing process, they chose to mature the blend in very charred Durmast oak casks formerly used for bourbon. This unique process releases spicy aromas that are both balanced and daring.

Tasting

Color: *golden with amber highlights.*
Nose: *spicy, sweet and piquant notes, from vanilla to pepper, ginger and cardamom, fade away to reveal fragrances of ripe tropical fruit.*
Palate: *balanced, complex and full-bodied, with strong spicy notes balanced out by hints of vanilla and sweet caramel.*
Finish: *intense, long with good persistence.*
Ideal: *straight up, on the rocks or in an Ichirouganaim cocktail, mixed with Mount Gay Rum Silver.*

Plantation
20th
Anniversary

Country: *Barbados*
Producer: *West Indies Rum Distillery*
ABV: *40%*
Bottle: *70 cl*
Typology: *Rum*

Production: *column and pot still distillation, first aged in casks in Barbados, then in small French oak cognac casks in France, followed by the assembly of prestigious aged rums, all originating from Barbados, ranging from 12 to 20 years.*

The company owned by Alexandre Gabriel, owner of the cognac house Maison Ferrand, has been in commercial relationships with the most important distilleries in the Caribbean for many years, to which it sold the casks used for aging its cognacs. A passionate connoisseur of the Caribbean, Alexandre discovered some small batches of extremely prestigious rum, of extraordinary quality and intensity, which were often destined for the personal consumption of the cellar Master or used to enrich other assemblies. This is how the Plantation brand was born. The selection includes Plantation 20th Anniversary, to celebrate the brand's twentieth anniversary, and three other rums, Gran Añejo, Five Years and Grande Réserve, all in the Signature Blend line, as well as the Vintage Collection rums from the Caribbean and Central America. One of the distinguishing characteristics of all Plantation rums is that they are aged twice, first in the Caribbean and then in the Cognac region in France. In the Caribbean, where the "angels' share" is an incredible 7% due to the tropical climate, the rum is aged for 8 to 10 years in American oak casks formerly used for bourbon, which give the rum notes of vanilla and coconut. The Plantation rums are then taken to Bonbonnet castle in Charente, where they are matured for anything between 2 to 10 years in small Pierre Ferrand cognac casks made of French oak, which infuse the rum with delicate hints of tannins. The second aging process gives the rum that touch of elegance and the finish that characterizes all Plantation rums.

Tasting
Color: *amber with mahogany highlights.*
Nose: *aromas of exotic fruit, including coconut, sugarcane, vanilla, candied citrus fruit, cocoa and smoky nuances.*
Palate: *evident hits of cinnamon, vanilla and cocoa. The long maturation period in oak casks leaves sensations of chocolate and marzipan.*
Finish: *complex and persistent.*
Ideal: *straight up.*

Gosling's Black Seal 80 Proof

Country: *Bermuda*
Producer: *Gosling family*
ABV: *40%*
Bottle: *70 cl*

Typology: *Rum*
Production: *a blend of three different Caribbean rums, aged from 3 to 6 years and then processed and blended in the Bermuda Islands.*

The Gosling family's history began in 1806, when James, the eldest son of William, merchant of wines and liqueurs, set off for America from the British port of Gravesend in Kent, with 10,000 pounds in his pocket. After travelling for more than two and a half years, he docked at the port of Saint George in Bermuda. Eighteen years later, together with one of his brothers, he rented a shop in the capital city, Hamilton. Three years later, the first Durmast oak casks of rum arrived in Bermuda, of various ages. In 1857, after a lot of experimenting with the assembly process, the rum that would later take the name Black Seal was put on sale. The composition, just like in the past, is a blend of three different Caribbean rums, aged between 3 and 6 years, which are then processed and blended in the Bermuda Islands. The name 80 Proof indicates that the rum has an ABV of 40%. The bouquet is enriched by notes of vanilla and caramel, which give this distillate a particularly distinctive style. Up until the First World War it was sold in bulk, then in Champagne bottles sealed with black wax, until arriving at the current style of the original label. Gosling's Black Seal, the only rum from the Bermuda Islands, is still owned by the Gosling family after over two hundred years. Bermuda's national cocktail, Dark 'n' Stormy, is made by mixing Gosling's Black Seal with Gosling's Ginger Beer.

Tasting

Color: *mahogany with coppery hues.*
Nose: *intense notes of butterscotch, vanilla and caramel.*
Palate: *rich, intricate, smooth and full-bodied.*
Finish: *rich and expressive.*
Ideal: *straight up or in a Caldera cocktail.*

N MODO FORT

LA HECHICERA

RON COLOMBIANO

40% vol   FINE AGED RUM FROM COLOMBIA   700ml ℮

La Hechicera Fine Aged Rum

Country: *Colombia*
Producer: *La Hechicera Company*
ABV: *40%*
Bottle: *70 cl*

Typology: *Colombian Ron*
Production: *blend of the best molasses-based rums, aged from 12 to 21 years using the Solera system.*

In Spanish, La Hechicera means "the enchantress," and this rum represents the seductive beauty and exuberance of the biodiversity along the coast of Colombia. After a careful selection of the raw base distillate, from the Caribbean, the rums are matured in Barranquilla, on the Colombian coast, using the Solera system and constantly supervised by *Maestros Roneros* (Master rum blender) Giraldo Mituoka. Giraldo, Cuban by birth, began his career as a sugarcane harvester in Cuba during the Cuban Revolution and, after years of hard work and fatigue, he earned the title of Maestro. The embargo against Cuba, making it impossible to sell rum in the United States, led the Cuban government to send some of its best *Maestros Roneros* to ally countries, with the aim of maturing the raw distillate produced in Cuba, bottling it as if it was made in another country and then selling it in the United States. This is how Giraldo Mituoka ended up in Colombia, combining his experience with that of the Riasco family, who for more than twenty years have been selecting the best raw distillates in the Caribbean. La Hechicera is a genuine rum, completely free of additives and without any additional sugar. Its smoothness is the result of decades of work; of the natural exchange that takes place between the incredible properties of the wood cask, the soul of the distillate and the passing of time.

Tasting

Color: *rich amber with a luminous glow.*
Nose: *characteristic and intriguing bouquet of citrus fruit, roasted coffee, tobacco, with a strong sensation of orange peel and a touch of fruitiness.*
Palate: *the flavor is vibrant, round and clean. It displays toasted and spicy notes.*
Finish: *harmonious and elegant.*
Ideal: *straight up or with a Bolivar Belicoso Campana cigar.*

Centenario Gran Legado 12 Años

Country: *Costa Rica*
Producer: *ATF*
ABV: *40%*
Bottle: *70 cl*

Typology: *Ron*
Production: *distillation in a multiple column still, maturation in white oak casks formerly used for bourbon.*

The creation process for Ron Centenario begins with the careful selection of native sugarcane. Costa Rica's tropical climate, favored by the volcanic soil, creates the ideal conditions for harvesting this plant. The harvest takes place every 15 months. After the stems are cut with apposite tools, the harvest is taken to the presses to extract the juice, which then undergoes fermentation with yeast. Once the fermentation process is completed, the liquid is then purified using a distillation process that refines and separates all the different parts. The Gran Legado selection is put into white Durmast oak casks, where it left to age for 12 years; the rum is then blended by the Master distiller before being bottled. Gran Legado pairs well with dishes like risotto with shrimps and candied orange or, even better, with typical Creole dishes like marinated pork. It is also ideal in desserts with mascarpone cheese or paired with Sachertorte.

Tasting

Color: *amber.*
Nose: *vanilla, leather, chocolate, ripe fruit like peaches and apricots.*
Palate: *it opens with a flavor of chocolate and tertiary notes of leather, honey, evolving into notes of ripe fruit with a slight hint of aniseed and licorice.*
Finish: *sweet but not sickly, warm, smooth and persistent, ending with spicy and toasted sensations.*
Ideal: *straight up, with a smooth medium-bodied cigar or chocolate with a cocoa percentage of less than 80%.*

Santiago de Cuba Carta Blanca

Country: *Cuba*
Producer: *Corporación Cuba Ron*
ABV: *38%*
Bottle: *70 cl*

Typology: *Ron*
Production: *distillation in a column alembic still, maturation in American white Durmast oak casks for 3 years.*

Starting from the 16th century, different methods to produce and blend Ron spread throughout the Antilles; in Cuba, thanks to the help of local and European technical innovations, an aromatic product was developed, with such an elegant taste that it took the name of *Ron Ligero* and became a rival to heavier distillates from other Caribbean countries. This distillation, aging and blending method which developed in Cuba, and in particular in Santiago de Cuba, continues to be the highest expression of the art of producing *Ron Ligero*. Ron Santiago de Cuba is made, aged and bottled exclusively in the homonymous city, in the first and oldest Cuban Ron distillery, dating back to 1862. Made with molasses, this rum is aged naturally, in carefully selected white Durmast oak casks, some of which, for the superior selections, have been in use for over 70 years. The heat and humidity of the Tropics naturally accelerate the evaporation of the alcohol and fusion with the woody substances. The entire production process is meticulously supervised by *Maestros Roneros* (Master rum blenders), who pass the art of blending the various assortments of Ron on to their descendants. Santiago de Cuba is the cultural capital of the Caribbean, where there is a mixture of Caribbean cultures.

Tasting

Color: *pale amber and transparent.*
Nose: *round with citrus and floral notes and delicate spicy hints.*
Palate: *light, dry, smooth with characteristic fruity aromas.*
Finish: *persistent.*
Ideal: *straight up, on the rocks or in a Cubanacan cocktail.*

RON de EL SALVADOR

CIHUATÁN

DISTILLED IN
EL SALVADOR

PRODUCED BY
LICORERA CIHUATÁN

40% ALC./VOL.

70 cl

SOLERA   SOLERA

RESERVA
RUM AGED IN BOURBON CASKS FOR 12 YEARS

WE BELIEVE IN THE KINDNESS AND WISDOM OF
OUR SUGARCANE. IT HAS TAUGHT US TO GROW TOWARDS
THE SUN AND TO CULTIVATE THE FRUITS
OF THE EARTH LIKE SOMETHING SACRED.

Cihuatán Solera 12 Reserva Especial

Country: *El Salvador*
Producer: *Licorera Cihuatán*
ABV: *40%*
Bottle: *70 cl*

Typology: *Aged Rum*
Production: *distillation in a multiple column still, matured for 12 years in casks formerly used for bourbon using the Solera system.*

Cihuatán is a pre-Columbian archaeological site of great historical importance, located in the Central American country of El Salvador. The city, where Aztec influences are clearly seen in the architecture, was built and inhabited by the indigenous Maya-Pipil between 900 and 1200 AD. The name of the city, meaning "place of the woman," derives from the shape of the nearby Guazapa volcano, which looks like the silhouette of a woman lying on her back. Licorera Cihuatán is the first and only distillery to produce quality rum made with sugarcane grown in El Salvador, and the production process is controlled from start to finish; from the sugarcane plants, right through to the bottled rum. The company is a subsidiary of the La Cabaña sugar refinery, founded over a century ago, which has played a fundamental role in the development of the area's community and culture. In honor of the ancestral ties with their homeland and ancient origins, the managers at Licorera decided to contribute part of the proceeds from the sale of the company's rums to the restoration of the historic site, where research and excavations are constantly on hold due to lack of funds. Aging the rum with the Solera system favors the evaporation of the distillate and the maturation of each cask. They use American oak casks formerly used for bourbon, which ensure a perfect balance between the delicate hints of wood and the sweetness of the rum. The label and bottle collar display a stylized image of Tlaloc, the Aztec god of rain and fertility.

Tasting

Color: *mahogany with copper hues.*
Nose: *a symphony of fragrances of molasses and brown sugar.*
Finish: *long, rich and expressive.*
Ideal: *straight up.*

Hampden Fire Velvet Overproof

Country: *Jamaica*
Producer: *Hussey family*
ABV: *63%*
Bottle: *70 cl*

Typology: *White Overproof Rum*
Production: *triple distillation in discontinuous copper alembic stills.*

Founded in Trelawny in 1753, Hampden Estate is one of the oldest sugar estates in Jamaica. Renowned in the world of Jamaican rums for its 100% pot still rums with an intense flavor, the company is still producing distillates that are the quintessence of rum. This is thanks to the molasses being fermented for a very long time, up to 2 weeks, typical of traditional production methods for Jamaican rum. No commercial yeasts are used, only those produced on the estate. In 2009, the Hussey family bought Hampden Estate and began to rebuild the distillery, part of which had been destroyed in previous years. Since the company's change in ownership, the rum has been bottled both as Rum-Fire, a white overproof rum (with a high concentration of alcohol), which is exceptionally smooth and a surprising evolution, although still traditional, and as Hampden Gold, with an ABV of 40% and produced according to ancient techniques. To produce Rum-Fire, the distillery buys quality molasses from Jamaican sugar refineries, selected according to the sugar content and the quality of the sugarcane harvest. The distillation process is supervised by Master distiller Winston Reid.

Tasting

Color: *clear and crystalline.*
Nose: *ample bouquet and lightly fruity aroma.*
Palate: *crisp flavor, surprisingly sweet with hints of pineapple and cashew nuts.*
Finish: *smooth, decisive and very persistent.*
Ideal: *on the rocks with a squeeze of lime.*

Worthy Park Rum-Bar White Overproof

Country: *Jamaica*
Producer: *Worthy Park*
ABV: *63%*
Bottle: *70 cl*

Typology: *Pure Single Rum*
Production: *discontinuous distillation in a double retort pot still.*

The Worthy Park Estate, founded in 1670, is located in the town of St. Catherine, in the heart of Jamaica, 60 kilometers north of Kingston. The distillery, run by just three different families over 340 years, produced rum from the onset, and can therefore be considered the oldest working distillery in the world. Today, it is a sugar refinery with a distillery that produces pure Jamaican style rum. The molasses produced on the estate undergoes two distinct types of fermentation, Light and Heavy, depending on the yeasts used, which are cultivated in Durmast oak vats. The discontinuous distillation, which takes place in a double retort alembic pot still, makes Rum-Bar a Pure Single Rum and a strong 65° overproof. It is an intense and extravagant rum, with a style that is typical of the island, explosive complexity and high alcohol by volume that is in perfect harmony with the true Jamaican style.

Tasting

Color: *clear and crystalline.*
Nose: *the powerful fragrances range from a decisive hint of sugarcane to aromas of exotic fruits and strong hints of lime.*
Palate: *lively and intense, dominated by the high alcoholic content.*
Finish: *extremely long, with sensations of chocolate and vanilla.*
Ideal: *on the rocks or in a Port Royal cocktail.*

Ron Añejo
BOTRAN
RESERVA BLANCA

Criado con la
más fina caña
de azúcar y
destilado localmente.

Elaborado bajo el
Sistema Solera con
rones especialmente
seleccionados.

40% vol   70 cle

PRODUCTO DE GUATEMALA

*Sistema
Solera*

Botran Reserva Blanca

Country: *Guatemala*
Producer: *Botran*
ABV: *40%*
Bottle: *70 cl*

Typology: *Ron Añejo*
Production: *after distillation it is aged with the Solera system, first in original oak casks and then in toasted oak casks formerly used for bourbon.*

At the beginning of the 20th century, five brothers belonging to the Botran family, from Burgos in Spain, settled in Guatemala. Having started with cultivating sugarcane, thanks to the ideal climate and volcanic soil, in 1939 they began to produce rum with the company Industria Licorera Quetzalteca. At the large Tulula sugarcane mill, situated on the southern coast of Guatemala, the sugarcane is cut and crushed to extract the juice, which then undergoes an evaporation process to obtain a sugarcane juice that is concentrated to 75% – known as *miel virgen* – as required by the Guatemala Protected Designation of Origin (PDO). To produce its rums, Botran ferments the concentrated sugarcane juice for 5 days, using a yeast strain created internally, which is capable of transforming sugars into substances that develop wonderful aromas and flavors in the final product. Like other rums, after distillation the Reserva is aged in oak casks, first in original oak and then in slightly toasted oak casks formerly used for bourbon, at an altitude of 2400 meters, using the Solera system (a process that involves mixing young and old rums by maturing them for a long time in white oak casks). Reserva Blanca is filtered using the active charcoal filtration method, thereby losing the amber pigment, yet maintaining the fruity flavor, with notes of wood, characteristic of aged rum.

Tasting

Color: *clear and crystalline.*
Nose: *notes of vanilla, butter, followed by sensations of leather, tobacco, almost a nuance of incense, with underlying hints of white pepper and dried fruit.*
Palate: *dry, smooth, warm and mellow, with notes of dried fruit, almond and hazelnut throughout.*
Finish: *rare complexity and structure for a white rum.*
Ideal: *on the rocks or in a Nahuatl cocktail.*

El Dorado 8 Years Old

Country: *Guyana*
Producer: *Demerara Distillers*
ABV: *40%*
Bottle: *70 cl*
Typology: *Single Blended Rum*

Production: *distillation in four traditional alembic stills, including the original Wooden Coffey still from the Enmore distillery and Port Mourant's double Wooden pot still, aged in Durmast oak casks formerly used for bourbon, followed by blending.*

Demerara Distillers, founded in 1670, produces the El Dorado brand and many other excellent rum selections. After the closure of the other eight distilleries in Guyana, the distillery, the only one to have remained operative in the country, acquired their alembic stills. The decision to keep the stills was extremely far-sighted on the part of the legendary chairman Yesu Persaud, as they are now able to continue producing different types of traditional rums. Today, El Dorado is a blend of several pot still rums and is therefore a mixture of these traditional products. The Demerara variety of sugarcane, excellent for producing Demerara sugar and rum, is cultivated on the shores of the Demerara River, in eastern Guyana. Naturally, the molasses is produced by the company and is also sold in most of the Caribbean. Demerara Distillers also produces its own yeasts for the fermentation of its rums. The distillery itself is called Diamond, and today it uses 13 alembic stills, made up of 9 different types. With each of these stills, Diamond produces one or more rums, defined as *marks*. The cask stock, one of the largest in the world with about 100,000 units, contains many different rums, some of which are extremely old, identifiable by the *marks* painted on the casks. The different El Dorado labels correspond to different blends of these *marks*. It is not just a style of rum, but a unique identity made up of a myriad of different characteristics, which when assembled give El Dorado rum its unique versatility.

Tasting
Color: *luminous with amber highlights.*
Nose: *notes of tobacco and caramel, followed by light hints of banana flambé.*
Palate: *smooth with a slightly sweet flavor and light woody sensations.*
Finish: *smooth with great persistence.*
Ideal: *straight up.*

Sol Tarasco Extra Aged Charanda

Country: *Mexico*
Producer: *Fabrica Casa Tarasco*
ABV: *43%*
Bottle: *70 cl*

Typology: *Guarapo Ancestral Rum*
Production: *continuous distillation in a single column still, no artificial additives, aged in casks for 12, 24 and 36 months, followed by blending.*

The Purepecha or Tarasca culture is a pre-Columbian culture which developed in the Mexican state of Michoacán. La Charanda, an artisan rum, is a traditional drink in this state, obtained by the column distillation of a fermented mash made with sugarcane juice. This distillate has existed since at least 1857, and its name, "red earth," pays homage to the place where the first distilleries were built. The sugarcane used to produce this rum grows an altitude of over 1300 meters, and the sugar content is higher than that present in varieties that grow at lower altitudes. Another fundamental element in the production process is the use of pure, high quality water, so as to obtain a polished product. This rum is certified with the "Extra Aged Charanda" Mexican Appellation of Origin. At the end of the maturation process, the Master blender selects casks that have been aged for 12, 24 and 36 months to produce a genuine artisan Charanda. During the aging process, the elements in this rum, made with concentrated sugarcane juice, create a particular type of fungus, *Cordyceps sinensin*, which has curative properties that, when tasting the rum, create a sensation of wellbeing, energy and vitality.

Tasting

Color: *pale amber, crystalline.*
Nose: *notes of honey, orange peel, vanilla and cinnamon.*
Palate: *opens with a strong sense of the rum's robustness.*
Finish: *velvety, persistent, extremely agreeable.*
Ideal: *straight up.*

Flor de Caña
Gran Reserva 7 Years Old

Country: *Nicaragua*
Producer: *Flor de Caña*
ABV: *40%*
Bottle: *70 cl*

Typology: *Ron*
Production: *distillation in a 6 column still, matured for 7 years in casks formerly used for bourbon.*

The nature of all five production stages – from the sugarcane to the molasses thereby obtained, from fermentation to aging and bottling, guarantees five-star authentic rums. The Pellas family, originally from Genoa, settled in Nicaragua at the end of the 19th century, creating the most important company in the country, and not just in the Ron industry. The company was established in 1890, in Chichigalpa, 120 kilometers from Managua. The initial idea was to create a vast sugarcane plantation, on land that is extremely conducive to this type of cultivation. In 1937, an independent company was established on the plantation, Compañia Licorera de Nicaragua, where there is the San Antonio sugar refinery, which produces sugarcane and molasses with 64% sugar, and the adjacent Flor de Caña distillery. Six columns produce a distillate that is then put in small 135-liter casks, formerly used for bourbon, which are then stored in *almacen* (warehouses) at a temperature of 28°C. Each year, 7% of the liquid evaporates. The Flor de Caña distillery owns 150,000 casks stored in the warehouses in Chichigalpa, one of the most important stocks in the world. Gran Reserva 7 Years Old is part of the Slow Aged line, together with Extra Seco 4 Years Old and Añejo Classico 5 Years Old.

Tasting
Color: *amber with mahogany hues.*
Nose: *a symphony of pleasing natural elements that go from vanilla to toasted coconut, followed by notes of red fruit like raisins and cherry.*
Palate: *dry, with notes of dark chocolate, candied orange and toasted walnuts.*
Finish: *long, rich and expressive.*
Ideal: *straight up.*

Ron
ABUELO
AÑEJO **7** AÑOS
RESERVA SUPERIOR

75cl   40% Alc./Vol.

Varela Hnos.
DESDE 1908
PRODUCT OF PANAMA

Ron Abuelo
7 Años

Country: *Panama*
Producer: *Varela Hermanos*
ABV: *38%*
Bottle: *70 cl*

Typology: *Ron*
Production: *multiple column distillation, aged for 7 years in specifically selected small white Durmast oak casks.*

Varela Hermanos S.A. exists thanks to Don José Varela Blanco, a young Spanish immigrant, who in 1908 moved to the new Republic of Panama and opened the first sugar refinery in Pesé L'Ingenio San Isidro. The town, founded in around the mid-18th century, lies in a fertile valley in the heart of Panama. Most of the town's approximately 10,000 inhabitants earn their livelihood through the cultivation of sugarcane. In 1936, complying with the wishes of his three eldest sons, Jose Manuel, Pliny and Julio, Don José began to distil virgin sugarcane juice to make liquors with. The company has always stood out for the extraordinary quality of its products, and from the onset it has been the leader in the market of distillates in Panama, with 1200 hectares producing approximately 75,000 tons of sugarcane and the distillation of both virgin juice and molasses. Today, Abuelo is run by the third generation of the family, producing approximately one million cases of rum every year, which represents 90% of the national spirit consumption. Ron Abuelo 7 Años is obtained from the fermentation of sugarcane molasses and aged for 7 years in small white Durmast oak casks, specifically selected for this product.

Tasting
Color: *straw yellow.*
Nose: *light hint of wood, with notes of desiccated fruit, including walnuts, evolving into a note of prunes.*
Palate: *fragrances of caramel, vanilla, followed by dried fruit and ending with notes of smoke.*
Finish: *extremely balanced and light on the palate with notes of dates and dried fruit, ending with notes of smoke, leather and tobacco.*
Ideal: *straight up or in a Bocas del Toro cocktail.*

Malteco Reserva del Fundador 20 Años

Country: *Guatemala*
Producer: *Botegas de America*
ABV: *41%*
Bottle: *70 cl*

Typology: *Ron Reserva*
Production: *artisan column distillation, aged for at least 20 years in 220-liter oak casks formerly used for bourbon.*

The history of Malteco began with its founder Marco Savio, who, during a trip from Guatemala to the Caribbean, decided to create the brand by putting an image of the Quetzal bird on the labels. He chose this bird with colored feathers up to one meter long, venerated in the Pre-Columbian era, as his lucky charm. Reserva del Fundador, like the other rums in the range, is made from concentrated virgin sugarcane honey extracted from high quality plants, according to the ancient art of *Maestros Roneros* (Master rum blenders), who for generations have handed down the formula for this ancient and valuable Guatemalan recipe, which is also verified by the Trade Association. The production process for making the Reserva begins with fermentation with high quality yeasts, followed by closely monitored column distillation and maturation in Durmast oak casks for 20 years, which takes place in the hills. The last stage involves the final selection, which determines the style of this limited product. The product range includes a 10-year-old Añejo Suave, a 15-year old Reserva Maya and a 25-year old Reserva Rare, bottled at the very peak of its maturity.

Tasting

Color: *intense amber with mahogany highlights.*
Nose: *notes of spices and tobacco, woody and toasted notes, with underlying hints of white pepper and dried fruit.*
Palate: *sweet, harmonious, balanced, round, for meditation.*
Finish: *spicy, sweet and very persistent.*
Ideal: *straight up, with a cigar or small toasted fruit.*

Zafra Master Reserve 21 Años

Country: *Panama*
Producer: *Zafra*
ABV: *40%*
Bottle: *70 cl*

Typology: *Ron*
Production: *continuous column distillation, maturation for 21 years in selected casks formerly used for bourbon.*

In Spanish, *zafra* means sugarcane harvest. This is the moment in which nature rewards people for their months of dedication and hard work. After the harvest and following the various stages of fermentation and distillation, the sugarcane becomes rum, which when carefully matured, depending on the production choices and type of casks used for aging, becomes aged rum. The founders of the Zafra brand worked with a top rum producer in Panama to create Zafra Master Reserve 21 Años, destined to be their most polished expression. From the onset, they decided to only use hand-picked sugarcane, transformed into high quality, grade A molasses that is then fermented with locally produced yeasts. After distillation, the aging process takes place exclusively in selected bourbon casks, under the watchful eye of the Master distiller, who, during the various stages of his creation, ensures that the rum is perfectly balanced and has great structure. Given the length of the maturation process, the casks are checked to make sure they are in optimum condition to hold the raw distillate. Before bottling, there is a final check at how each cask has interacted with the rum, before creating small batches of the limited edition.

Tasting

Color: *dark amber with coppery hues.*
Nose: *a dominant note of Durmast oak that balances perfectly with the elegant hints of dark fruit, spices and a note of menthol.*
Palate: *ample and smooth with decisive, yet not overbearing, notes of wood.*
Finish: *long, bursting with creamy hints of wood.*
Ideal: *straight up, with chocolate with a cocoa percentage of 70% or in a Wari Wari cocktail.*

Ron Millonario Reserva Especial 15 Años

Country: *Peru*
Producer: *Rossi & Rossi Treviso*
ABV: *40%*
Bottle: *70 cl*

Typology: *Ron Reserva*
Production: *column distillation in three stages, aged for up to 15 years in Durmast oak casks formerly used for bourbon and French and Spanish wines, using the Solera system.*

In around 1922, Don Rolando Piera de Castillo, a Peruvian landowner, bought the sugar refinery and the immense sugarcane plantations of the Hacienda Agrícola de Chiclayo. After graduating in chemical engineering in England, his eldest son Augusto returned to Peru with a special machine for processing sugar and an alembic still for producing distillates. He invented a recipe from the raw materials, which he handed down to future generations, and today it still rests in the casks formerly used for American bourbon and Spanish and French wines. Ron Millonario, produced in the region of Lambayeque, has been owned by the Rossi & Rossi company since 2004, when it bought the brand and exclusive rights to the entire stock of existing products. Two types of sugarcane are used, both native, and the yeasts used in the fermentation process are also local. Distillation takes place in three stages: the first separates the alcohol from the water in the historic alembic still; the second involves the depuration or polishing of the alcohols; during the third stage, the heads and tails are removed. At this point, the distillate is decanted into Durmast oak casks and left to age for up to 15 years, using the Solera system, giving the rum its consistent style and velvety smoothness. Each bottle is wrapped inside a hand-woven cover made of toquilla fiber, cultivated in a small town in the North of Peru.

Tasting

Color: *amber with walnut brown hues.*
Nose: *the fragrances go from mature plums and figs to coconut, dates and caramel, evolving into cocoa and cloves.*
Palate: *compact, thick, yet perfectly balanced. Deep, pleasantly sweet, with complex notes of fig, dates, butterscotch and cloves, combined with hints of dark chocolate.*
Finish: *gentle, great drinkability, very persistent.*
Ideal: *straight up, with chocolate or in an El Coronel cocktail.*

Don Q Añejo

Country: *Puerto Rico*
Producer: *Destilería Serrallés*
ABV: *42%*
Bottle: *70 cl*
Typology: *Blended Rum*

Production: *multiple column distillation for light rum and single column distillation for heavy rum, aged for between 3 and 8 years in Durmast oak casks formerly used for bourbon, followed by blending.*

Founded in 1861 by Don Juan Serrallés, in a small sugarcane plantation called "Hacienda Mercedita," today Don Q is still a family owned company that is faithful to its over 150 years of history. It selects only the best molasses, using pure water from the River Inabòm and distilling and aging its rums in Puerto Rico, as required by the product specification. Don Q has two distinguishing characteristics: the eco-sustainability of its distillation plants and its desire to only produce Puerto Rican Rum, without the addition of any kind of sugar, aromas, glycerol, musts or syrups. Furthermore, all its rums are distilled and aged in Puerto Rico, as required by the product specification. This is the rum that originally inspired the Piña Colada cocktail in 1954, at the Caribe Hilton in San Juan. The company's choice to distill the rum in two different stills and age it in American white Durmast oak casks, together with the complete absence of additional ingredients, has made Don Q rums famous for being clean and elegant.

Tasting
Color: *pale amber.*
Nose: *intense fragrances ranging from the sweet spiciness of cinnamon to piquant notes of pepper, softening out into sophisticated tertiary notes of hazelnut, vanilla, cocoa and ending with hints of dried fruit and molasses.*
Palate: *smooth, round, with an aftertaste of molasses, vanilla and sensations which, together with the vanilla, soften the bouquet and take the edge off the alcohol burn.*
Finish: *dry, aromatic, with good persistence.*
Ideal: *straight up, with a San Cristobal de La Habana El Principe Minutos cigar or in a Cueva de L'Indio cocktail, mixed with Don Q Cristal rum.*

Brugal Extra Viejo

Country: *Dominican Republic*
Producer: *Edrington Group and the Brugal family*
ABV: *38%*
Bottle: *70 cl*
Typology: *Ron*

Production: *double distillation in a continuous column still, maturation for over 8 years in American white Durmast oak casks formerly used for bourbon and Spanish red Durmast oak casks formerly used for sherry.*

The bond between the Brugal family and the Dominican Republic began 5 generations ago, in 1888, when Don Andres founded the distillery. Today, as back then, the family produces Ron, and the entire production process takes places in the Dominican Republic: from the selection of the raw material right through to bottling. The La Romana and San Pedro sugar refineries supply the distillery with molasses, and the sugarcane used to produce the sugar, 100% Dominican, comes exclusively from 8000 hectares of locally cultivated crops. Double distillation in a continuous column still produces a liquid with an alcohol by volume of approximately 95°, subsequently lowered, which must then rest for at least one year in the cask to become Ron. During the aging process, the role of the *Maestros Roneros* (Master rum blenders) Jassill and Gustavo, is decisive. They are responsible for checking that the casks, a mixture of American white Durmast oak bourbon casks and Spanish red Durmast oak sherry casks, always produce a consistent liquid. Part of the distillery's energy requirement is met by a biofuel, obtained using the waste produced during the distillation process, significantly reducing CO_2 emissions.

Tasting

Color: *dark amber, bright and clear.*
Nose: *a symphony of natural element's opening with notes of wood and followed by aromas of dried fruit, almonds, cocoa, vanilla, orange peel, caramel and molasses.*
Palate: *an elegant flavor with notes of vanilla, caramel and honey, followed by hints of spiciness and pure cocoa.*
Finish: *after the initial warm notes, it is persistent on the palate with a faint hint of pepper.*
Ideal: *straight up.*

Presidente Marti 15 Años Solera

Country: *Dominican Republic*
Producer: *Oliver & Oliver*
ABV: *40%*
Bottle: *70 cl*
Typology: *Artesanal Ron*

Production: *distillation carried out in several stages in a continuous column still, maturation, first in new French Durmast oak casks, then transferred to casks formerly used for Pedro Ximenes sherry for 15 years.*

The origins of this rum lie in the Cuban roots of the Oliver family, now settled in the Dominican Republic. José Martí Julián Pérez was a politician, writer and leader of the movement for Cuban independence in the mid-19th century. Today, he is considered one of the greatest national heroes in Cuba. One of his most famous works is a poem in *Versos Sencillos* (Simple Verses), which inspired the lyrics of one of the most loved songs in Cuba: "Guantanamera." This romantic bolero serenade, dedicated to a *guajira guantanamera* (a peasant girl from Guantanamo), is set in the end of the 19th century, at the height of the fight for independence in the then Spanish colony. After the artisan distillation process, the rum obtained from sugarcane juice and concentrated syrup undergoes several stages in different types of casks, using the Solera system. The rum is first put in new French Durmast oak casks, which give it a spicy component and tannins. It is then transferred to casks formerly used for Pedro Ximenes sherry, in which there is a remnant of wine that over time will mix with the rum, giving it color and the characteristic fruity aroma. The combination of different aged rums and maturation techniques gives this rum its smoothness and depth.

Tasting

Color: *pale mahogany with hues of amber.*
Nose: *intense, persistent fragrance, displaying notes of caramel and fruit.*
Palate: *rich, exuberant and harmonious, with hints of wood.*
Finish: *after the initial warm notes, it is persistent on the palate with a faint hint of pepper.*
Ideal: *straight up or with a Cuban cigar.*

Admiral Rodney St. Lucia Rum

Country: *Saint Lucia*
Producer: *St. Lucia Distillers*
ABV: *40%*
Bottle: *70 cl*

Typology: *Extra Old Rum*
Production: *continuous distillation, aged for 12 years in American Durmast oak casks formerly used for bourbon, followed by blending.*

Admiral Rodney Rum commemorates the British Admiral who defeated the French fleet in the Battle of the Saints in 1782. The small St. Lucia Distillers has been producing extremely prestigious rums on the beautiful Caribbean island of Saint Lucia since 1972, adhering to the most important British rum production traditions, yet at the same time experimenting with new distillation methods. After the molasses has undergone a long fermentation process, which takes place in open vats with the use of wild yeasts, the liquid is distilled in both modern column stills and traditional discontinuous stills. The rum is aged in American Durmast oak casks, previously used to produce bourbon, sherry or cognac. The combined use of different stills and the various types of casks used for aging, produces a rum that is rich in aromas and extremely well-balanced, qualities for which the Saint Lucia Distillers is famous throughout the world. Each batch of Admiral Rodney is matured separately in American Durmast oak casks that have previously contained Jim Beam or Jack Daniels; currently, the rum is left to mature for about 12 years, but in the future the distillery intends to arrive at an average of 15. When the Master distiller decides that the right level of maturation has been reached, he creates the blend by adding reserve rums that have been aged for longer, still available in the distillery, each time with the intention of making one of the best rums in the world, after which the rum is bottled.

Tasting
Color: *bright amber with mahogany highlights.*
Nose: *complex with sweet fruity notes of honey, prunes, raisins and toasted Durmast oak.*
Palate: *concentrated, complex, with notes of crème caramel and hints of vanilla, spices and chocolate.*
Finish: *well-balanced and harmonious, with an exceptionally long finish.*
Ideal: *straight up.*

Angostura 1919

Country: *Trinidad & Tobago*
Producer: *Angostura*
ABV: *40%*
Bottle: *70 cl*

Typology: *Gold Rum*
Production: *distillation in a column alembic still, aged for a minimum of 8 years in casks formerly used for bourbon, followed by blending, for which the youngest rum used is 8 years old.*

The history of the House of Angostura began in 1824, when German doctor Johan Gottlieb Benjamin Siegert, Surgeon General of the Venezuelan army, created a blend of aromatic herbs called "Aromatic Amargo." This product subsequently became famous worldwide as Angostura bitters.

There is no doubt that the House of Angostura has remained famous for its bitters, but today it is also well-known for its rums. These authentic Caribbean style products are made with high quality molasses, using the distillery's own yeasts cultures for fermentation. Distillation takes place in a column alembic still, under the expert supervision of the Master distiller, John Georges. The rums are aged in Durmast oak casks formerly used for bourbon, and then blended. This is how Angostura 1919 is made; created with rums of different ages matured entirely in the climate of Trinidad & Tobago, for a minimum of 8 years. The name refers to the casks of rum dated 1919, which were saved from a huge fire that destroyed the Government Rum Bond in 1932. This rum blend became known as 1919, and Angostura decided to reuse the name.

Tasting

Color: *clear and golden.*

Nose: *the initial fragrances are dominated by vanilla, which then melts into caramel, honey and a buttery note, followed by aromas of ripe apricots, bananas, brown sugar and molasses. It ends with notes of candied orange and sweet spices, which evolve into milk chocolate. Very smooth and gentle.*

Palate: *on tasting, it has a medium body and is fairly dry, with the orange flavor blending with light tobacco, followed by vanilla, a note of butter, cinnamon and banana-flavored chocolate. Not very complex, yet elegant and enjoyable.*

Finish: *not very persistent, an elegant style with an aftertaste of chocolate, sweet spices, orange and tobacco.*

Ideal: *straight up or in a Huevos cocktail.*

Diplomático
Reserva
Exclusiva

Country: *Venezuela*
Producer: *Destilerías Unidas*
ABV: *40%*
Bottle: *70 cl*
Typology: *Blended Rum*
Production: *distillation of 60 different rums in old copper pot stills for heavy rums, which make up 80% of the product range, in column stills and Batch Kettles for the remaining 20% of light and medium-bodied rums. Matured for a maximum of 12 years in small Durmast oak casks formerly used for bourbon and malt-whisky, then mixed in one blend*

The Destilerías Unidas was founded in 1959, in the large area of fertile countryside near the town of Barquisimeto, at the foot of the Andes. The town is in the region of Lara, considered one of the most prestigious areas for the cultivation of sugarcane, and is close to the Terepaima National Park, from where the distillery gets the water it uses in the distillation process, taken from 50-60-meter deep wells. At the end of the 1990s, a group of Venezuelan entrepreneurs bought the distillery and the land used to grow sugarcane, with the help of José Rafael Ballesteros, whose family already owned an important company in the rum industry. Reserva Exclusiva, symbol product of the Diplomático line, owes its name to Don Juancho Nieto Mendelez, who, at the end of the 19th century, started an impressive collection of spirits which he loved buying and sharing with his friends: the collection was known as "the Ambassador's Reserve." This rum is made with the purest sugarcane honey (concentrated sugarcane juice) and a smaller percentage of molasses. This elegant, complex tasting rum owes its fame to the combination of different distillation techniques and the exceptional storage method in barriques, to its full-body and excellent balance of the blend, created by Master distiller Tito Codero, who has worked at the distillery for decades, ensuring, with almost maniacal care, a product par excellence.

Tasting

Color: *amber with golden highlights.*
Nose: *complex with notes of orange peel, ripe fruit, followed by chocolate, maple syrup and then hints of cinnamon, walnuts and licorice.*
Palate: *sweet with notes of toffee, ripe bananas, orange, followed by notes of walnut and hazelnut.*
It has an aftertaste of dark chocolate mixed with nutmeg and brown sugar.
Finish: *seductive, very persistent.*
Ideal: *straight up, with dark chocolate with a cocoa percentage of between 90% and 100%, or with a cigar.*

Roble Viejo Extra Añejo

Country: *Venezuela*
Producer: *Rones Añejos de Venezuela*
ABV: *40%*
Bottle: *70 cl*
Typology: *Ron Viejo*

Production: *distillation in a 5-column alembic still, aged for 8 years in American Durmast oak casks formerly used for bourbon, followed by blending with 8 to 12-year reserve rums.*

Ron Roble is created and produced by the chemical engineer Giorgio Melis. In 1967, after distilling and aging Pampero rum for 26 years and over 50 years of experience in the production of rum, he decided to leave the above-mentioned brand and establish Rones Añejos de Venezuela, a company specialized in aging, assembling and selling sugarcane-based distillates. His inspiration and dedication have led to the production of high-profile products like Roble Viejo Extra Añejo and Roble Viejo Ultra Añejo, which also mature for 12 years in old Pedro Ximenes sherry casks, the blend of which is made up exclusively of aged rums of the same vintage. Extra Añejo is obtained from sugarcane molasses and is distilled in a 5-column alembic still, which makes it possible to select just the heart of the distillate. It is then matured for a minimum of 8 years in American Durmast oak casks formerly used for bourbon, without being topped up. The blend is a mixture of 8 to 12-year reserve rums from selected batches, aged in Durmast oak casks once used for bourbon or sometimes scotch.

Tasting

Color: *amber with mahogany highlights.*
Nose: *hints of sweet spices like vanilla and cinnamon, followed by a strong note of caramel.*
Palate: *robust flavor with character.*
Finish: *vanillary, delicately spicy, persistent.*
Ideal: *straight up, with sparkling water it pairs well with Habanos cigars and chocolate.*

"Exotic" Rums

Ryoma Rhum Japonais Vieilli 7 Ans

Savanna Grand Arôme Lontan Blanc

Vanilla Dzama Vieux 10 Ans

The Arcane Extraroma 12 Years Old

Saint Aubin Premium White Rum

In this section, we present a few brands with exotic origins: from Madagascar to Mauritius, Île de la Réunion and Japan, places where sugarcane and those who transform it create extremely interesting rums. The Kikusui Shuzo distillery dedicates Ryoma Rhum, made with sugarcane juice and aged for 7 years in American Durmast oak casks, to Sakamoto Ryōma, a Japanese Samurai from the same city as the distillery, who played a fundamental role in the Meiji Restoration.

On Île de la Réunion, Savanna produces Grand Arôme, a rum blanc obtained by prolonged fermentation processes, which evokes memories of 18th century artisan products. From the extraordinary island of Madagascar, there is a distillate that is notable for its 10-year maturation period, Vanilla Dzama, flavored with a whole Madagascan vanilla pod. We have included two sugarcane juice-based rums from Mauritius: Arcane Extraroma, a Solera rum that is aged for 12 years in casks with low tannin content, and a Saint Aubin premium quality Rhum Agricole, obtained from the heart of the distillate, made by a producer with a deep-seated ecological philosophy, based in the south of the island.

RYOMA
Rhum Japonais
Vieilli 7 ans / Fût de chêne

黒糖酒

さとうきびのお酒

70cl 40% vol

Ryoma Rhum Japonais Vieilli 7 Ans

Country: *Japan*
Producer: *Kikusui Shuzo*
ABV: *40%*
Bottle: *70 cl*

Typology: *Rhum*
Production: *discontinuous distillation in an alembic still, aged in American Durmast oak casks.*

The Kikusui Shuzo distillery is in Kochi, on Shikoku Island, in the south of the Japanese archipelago. Sugarcane cultivation is diffused in the Land of the Rising Sun, especially in Kochi, where it has been famous for its quality since the beginning of the 20th century. The rum's name is inspired by Sakamoto Ryōma, a Japanese samurai born in Kochi, who played an important role in the movement that overturned the Tokugawa Shogunate during the Bakumasu period, giving rise to the period known as the Meiji Restoration. Using its own plantations, the Kikusui distillery decided to develop a rum inspired by the mastery of Japanese distillers, using the best production techniques and related equipment, but most importantly, made exclusively with fresh sugarcane juice, so as to obtain a prestigious quality rum. It decided to use a discontinuous distillation technique, then only maturing the heart of the distillate for 7 years in American Durmast oak casks, controlling the quality of the product in the final blending stage.

Tasting
Color: *straw yellow.*
Nose: *opens with floral notes of rose, evolving into aromas typical of sugarcane juice-based rums, vanilla, mango, passion fruit, followed by honey, hazelnuts and white truffle.*
Palate: *round, sweet and delicate with notes of chocolate, apricot and a spicy note of ginger, very complex.*
Finish: *long, captivating, persistent.*
Ideal: *straight up.*

*Savanna
Grand
Arôme
Lontan
Blanc*

Country: *Île de la Réunion (France)*
Producer: *Savanna*
ABV: *40%*
Bottle: *70 cl*
Typology: *Rhum Traditionnel*

Production: *molasses distilled in alembic stills with no more than 2 columns, maturation in 400-liter French casks formerly used for cognac and calvados.*

The volcanic island of Île de la Réunion, a French overseas department like the French Antilles, is in the Southern hemisphere of the Indian Ocean, east of Madagascar. The island, with its wild and exuberant nature, is a major producer of sugar and has three large refineries. Savanna selects the sugarcane with which to make its rum and produces both the raw materials, sugarcane juice and molasses, the only distillery in the world to do so, using the latter to develop the Grand Arôme style alongside the regular Traditionnel. The molasses is fermented for over a week, making it possible to obtain a rum that is extremely rich in congeners, the non-ethanol components responsible for the aromas. Master Distiller Laurent Broc, Savanna's deus ex machina, is one of the greatest rum experts in the world, mainly because he knows all the typologies and carries out extremely eclectic experiments. Laurent has also perfected the aging process, designing and building a structure of ducts and valves that connect all the casks containing the younger rums, so as to transfer the liquid frequently into large casks during the first 18 months, thereby creating balance and ventilation. Laurent has approximately a thousand casks for old rums, all of French origin, with an average capacity of 400 liters, and he also manages dozens of casks formerly used for cognac, port, madeira, sherry, muscatel and calvados. He uses these for the finish (sometimes very long) of the different rums he produces, creating dozens of extremely interesting combinations, which he bottles in a single keg, in limited editions.

Tasting
Color: *transparent, bright.*
Nose: *multifaceted, with aromas of orange blossom, dates, dried figs, a delicate sensation of chestnut honey, walnuts and vanilla.*
Palate: *round, with some of the aromas perceived on the nose continuing in the long aftertaste.*
Finish: *rich, expressive, with the floral notes returning together with a salty sensation.*

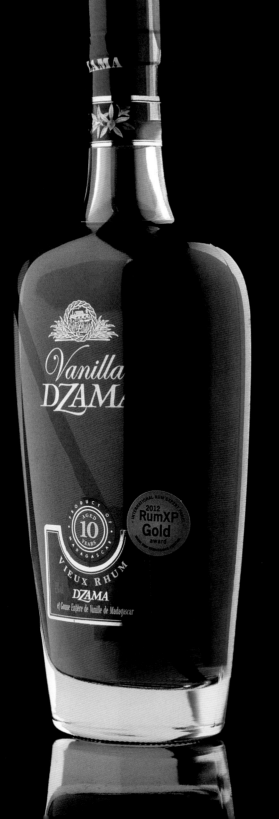

Vanilla Dzama Vieux 10 Ans

Country: *Madagascar*
Producer: *Vidzar*
ABV: *43%*
Bottle: *70 cl*

Typology: *Vieux Rhum*
Production: *continuous distillation in a single column still, no artificial additives, aged for 10 years in casks formerly used for whisky.*

In 1980, Lucien Fohine, fascinated by the places and scents of Madagascar, decided to create rums which expressed the aromas and flavors on the island of Nosy Be, nicknamed the "Island of Perfumes." The production process he used was influenced by both the culture of cognac – he knew how important where the sugarcane grew was –, and the Scottish art of cask finishing, i.e. secondary maturation in specific wood casks. Lucien chose the Dzamadzar sugar refinery/distillery to make his rums, founded on Nosy Be in 1929, using different batches and harvesting areas for the sugarcane, which was surrounded by other local plantations like the much-prized Madagascan vanilla, cloves, ylang ylang and pepper. It is no coincidence that the aromas of these plants have a positive influence on the rum, with delicate fragrances on the nose, using the same principle as wine, which when poured into the glass bursts with the fragrances of the fruit cultivated close to the vineyard. The minerality induced by the island's volcanic soil is important in this line of rums. Today, Dzama is the most important brand of the company Vidzar in Antananarive, which has become a flourishing business in Madagascar. Since 1996, it has been run by Franck Fohine, Lucien's son, who continues to transmit the true essence of the culture of this unique country. The rum is made with molasses, so as to produce a product that is more robust and ready for aging, which takes place inside Durmast oak casks formerly used for Scotch whisky. Before bottling, the distillate is filtered five times through different filters to remove all the impurities. Finally, a vanilla pod is put inside the bottle.

Tasting

Color: *amber with mahogany highlights.*
Nose: *opens with evident notes of vanilla, followed by those of caramel, banana, chocolate.*
Palate: *initially smooth and fairly round, followed by a clear sensation of its robustness and toasted notes accompanied by vanilla and red plum.*
Finish: *persistent with notes of vanilla.*
Ideal: *straight up.*

The Arcane Extraroma 12 Years Old

Country: *Mauritius*
Producer: *Odevie distillery*
ABV: *41%*
Bottle: *70 cl*

Typology: *Amber Rum*
Production: *aged 12 years with the Solera system, in Durmast oak casks with low tannin content so as not to mask the notes of fresh sugarcane.*

For more than two centuries, Mauritius, an island in the south-western Indian Ocean, has been known as an area particularly suited for growing sugarcane and producing rum and sugar. The balance between the frequent rainfall, the characteristics of the Archipelago's volcanic soil, rich in minerals, and its incredible fertility, creates the ideal environment for the cultivation of sugarcane. Arcane Extraroma is the result of the combination of the island's sugarcane, the pure sugarcane juice and the art of Master distiller Thibault de la Fournière. This amber rum, a blend of young and old rums, is left to age for 12 years in lightly toasted American oak casks, so as not to mask the fresh notes of sugarcane, using the Solera system. It combines fresh aromas of sugarcane and very smooth aromas, which at the same time are as complex as those of an old rum. What makes this rum unique, is its incredible aromatic richness, given to the quality of Mauritian sugarcane. The dark, square bottle (clear glass for Dog Crush white rum) was chosen to protect the precious nectar inside. The design of the labels, which plays with black, gold details and touches of mint green, emphasizes the aura of alchemy and mystery that surround this rum, transmitting Thibault de la Fournière's vision.

Tasting

Color: *deep amber.*
Nose: *opulent, with notes of exotic fruit and pastries, followed by hints of fresh sugarcane, typical of juice-based rums and spicy hints given to the Solera maturation.*
Palate: *smooth, incredible profusion of flavors, with exotic fruit like banana and coconut softening out into chocolate, vanilla and dried fruit.*
Finish: *spicy, long and persistent.*
Ideal: *straight up.*

Saint Aubin
Premium White Rum

Country: *Mauritius*
Producer: *Saint Aubin*
ABV: *50%*
Bottle: *70 cl*

Typology: *White Rum*
Production: *made with pure sugarcane juice, distillation in a traditional copper column alembic still.*

Extending across the undulating hillsides in the south of Mauritius, Saint Aubin's fields have been planted with sugarcane since 1819. Later, vanilla was planted on the estate and they built a distillery to produce rum. The Saint Aubin estate, which takes its name from one of its first owners, produces Mauritian rum distilled directly from fresh sugarcane juice. The sugarcane is harvested by hand and sent to the mill, where it is gently squeezed to extract the first juice, known in Mauritius as *Fangourin*. After distillation, only the heart of the distillate is kept, which is diluted with pure spring water, with low mineral content, from the Bois Chéri plantation. The microclimate is extremely favorable for the cultivation of sugarcane, thanks to the generous rainfall, abundant sunshine and volcanic soil, which, together with the company's deep-seated ecological philosophy, produce authentic rums.

Tasting
Color: *clear and crystalline.*
Nose: *floral fragrance with notes of vanilla, honey, fresh sugarcane juice, closing with a sensation of olive pâté.*
Palate: *displays a warm body thanks to its 50°, with a rich and generous taste.*
Finish: *generous and persistent.*
Ideal: *on the rocks or in a Ilha Do Cerne cocktail.*

Cocktails

Anse
la Cuve

Cubanacan

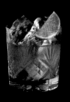

Baron
Samedi

#Cueva
de l'Indio

Bocas
del Toro

El
Coronel

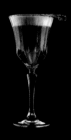

Caldera

Huevos

Ichirouganaim

Papillon

Ilha
do Cerne

Port
Royal

Leopold
Heritage

Wari
Wari

Nahuatl

Bartending Team:

Fabio Bacchi – *Bar Manager*
Carlo Simbula – *Head Bartender*
Vincenzo Losappio – *Bartender*
Alessandro Impagnatiello – *Bartender*

Anse la Cuve

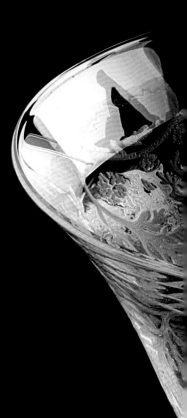

Ingredients

3 cl (1 fl oz) Père Labat 59
1 cl (0.3 fl oz) Mezcal Illegal Joven
0.5 cl (0.15 fl oz) Habanero cordial-lemon verbena
2 cl (0.6 fl oz) Cocchi Rosa

Method: stir and strain • Glass: Coupette
Garnish: lemon zest

Preparation

Put the ingredients in a mixing glass.
Stir gently, add ice cubes and stir again.
Pour into a cocktail coupe and squeeze lemon zest
over the top to release the essential oils into the drink.

Baron Samedì

Ingredients

4 cl (1.3 fl oz) Clairin Casimir 3.1
1/4 whole lime
1 dash Absinthe Duplais
1 dash Bob's Grapefruit Bitters
0.75 cl (0.25 fl oz) Orgeat syrup

Method: build • Glass: Old fashioned
Garnish: lime

Preparation

Prepare directly in the glass. Squeeze the wedge of lime into the glass, add the other ingredients and stir. Fill with ice and stir again. Garnish with a wedge of lime.

Bocas del Toro

Ingredients

3 cl (1 fl oz) Ron Abuelo 7 Años • 0.5 cl (0.15 fl oz) Brandy
Lepanto • 1.5 cl (0.5 fl oz) Tio Pepe Sherry Fino •
2 barspoons smoked date syrup
Top-up: Champagne

Method: shake
Glass: Flute
Garnish: dates

Preparation

Put all of the ingredients, apart from the Champagne, in the shaker. Mix them together, add ice and shake. Strain into an iced flute and top-up with Champagne. Garnish with a date skewer.

Caldera

Ingredients

5 cl (1.7 fl oz) Gosling's Black Seal • 1 cl (0.3 fl oz) Timut pepper syrup •
1 cl (0.3 fl oz) yuzu juice • 1 cl (0.3 fl oz) pineapple and rhubarb shrub •
0.5 cl (0.15 fl oz) Glenrothes Whisky Sherry Cask Reserve
Top-up: bergamot soda

Method: shake
Glass: Glass goblet
Garnish: dehydrated pineapple

Preparation

Put all of the ingredients in a shaker, stir and shake with ice. Pour into a wine glass filled with ice. Garnish with a thin slice of dehydrated pineapple.

Cubanacan

Ingredients

3.5 cl (1.2 fl oz) Santiago de Cuba Carta Blanca
1 cl (0.3 fl oz) Fifty Pounds Gin
1.5 cl (0.5 fl oz) lime and yellow grapefruit juice
1.5 cl (0.5 fl oz) cardamom-cinnamon honey syrup

Method: shake • Glass: Canchanchara glass
Garnish: lime

Preparation

Put all of the ingredients in a shaker, stir and shake with ice. Pour into a typical terracotta cup filled with ice cubes, or alternatively into a short tumbler.
Garnish with a lime wheel.

#Cueva
de l'Indio

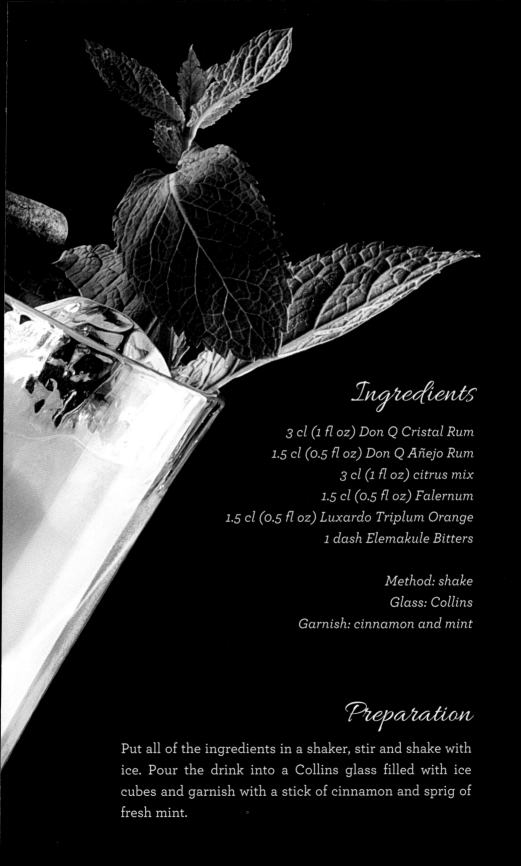

Ingredients

3 cl (1 fl oz) Don Q Cristal Rum
1.5 cl (0.5 fl oz) Don Q Añejo Rum
3 cl (1 fl oz) citrus mix
1.5 cl (0.5 fl oz) Falernum
1.5 cl (0.5 fl oz) Luxardo Triplum Orange
1 dash Elemakule Bitters

Method: shake
Glass: Collins
Garnish: cinnamon and mint

Preparation

Put all of the ingredients in a shaker, stir and shake with ice. Pour the drink into a Collins glass filled with ice cubes and garnish with a stick of cinnamon and sprig of fresh mint.

El
Coronel

Ingredients

4 cl (1.3 fl oz) Ron Millonario 15 Años
1 cl (0.3 fl oz) Pisco infused with Kaffir lime leaves
2 dashes Amargo Chungo
2 cl (0.6 fl oz) red Vermouth Macchia

Method: stir and strain
Glass: Champagne coupe
Garnish: star anise

Preparation

Put the ingredients in a mixing glass. Stir gently, add ice cubes and stir again. Pour into a Champagne coupe and add one ice cube to the glass. Garnish with star anise.

Huevos

Ingredients

2.5 cl (0.85 fl oz) yellow grapefruit juice
2 cl (0.6 fl oz) Parang Masala syrup
5 cl (1.7 fl oz) Angostura 1919

Method: shake
Glass: Champagne coupe
Garnish: raspberries, mint

Preparation

Put all of the ingredients in a shaker,
stir and shake with ice.
Pour into a Champagne coupe, garnish
with raspberries and a sprig of mint.

Ichirouganaim

Ingredients

2.5 cl (0.85 fl oz) lime juice • 1 cl (0.3 fl oz) Mount Gay Black Barrel •
4 cl (1.3 fl oz) Mount Gay Silver • 1.5 cl (0.5 fl oz) Dan Shen sage syrup •
0.5 cl (0.15 fl oz) Botanist Gin

Method: shake
Glass: Old fashioned
Garnish: sage leaf
and redcurrants

Preparation

Put all of the ingredients in a
shaker, stir and shake with
ice. Pour into an old fashioned
glass filled with ice cubes.
Garnish with a sage leaf and
sprig of redcurrants.

Ilha do Cerne

Ingredients

3 cl (1 fl oz) Saint Aubin White Rum • 2.5 cl (0.85 fl oz) lime juice •
2 cl (0.6 fl oz) sugar syrup • 1.5 cl (0.5 fl oz) Arangiu Liqueur
Top-up: IPA beer

Method: shake
Glass: Wine glass
Garnish: blackberries

Preparation

Put all of the ingredients, except for the beer, in a shaker; stir and shake with ice. Pour into a wine glass filled with ice and top-up with beer. Garnish with a blackberry skewer.

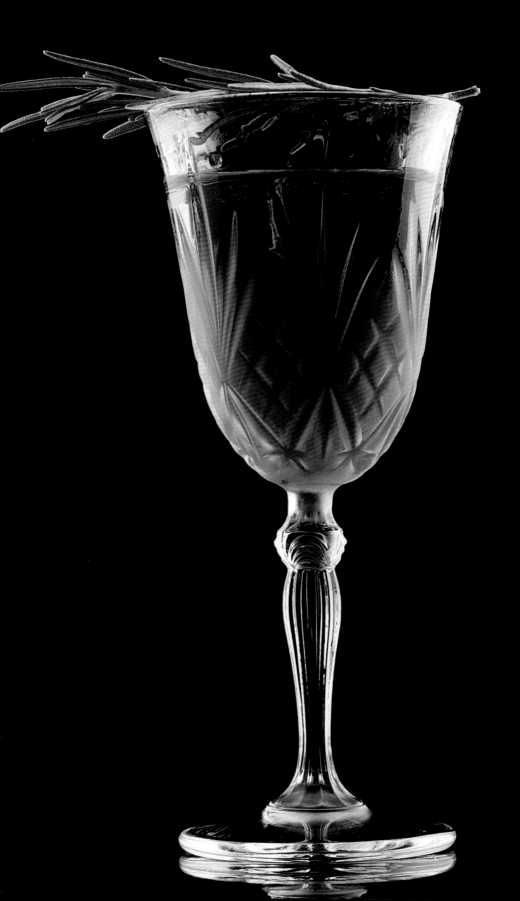

Leopold Heritage

Ingredients

2 cl (0.6 fl oz) Reimonenq Cuvée Spéciale Blanc Centenaire 50°
1.5 cl (0.5 fl oz) white hibiscus and lime cordial
2.5 cl (0.85 fl oz) Calvados Dupont Hors d'Age
1 cl (0.3 fl oz) Ruby Port

Method: stir and strain • Glass: Cocktail coupe
Garnish: rosemary

Preparation

Put the ingredients in a mixing glass. Stir gently, add ice
cubes and stir again. Pour into a cocktail coupe.
Garnish with a sprig of rosemary.

Ingredients

5 cl (1.7 fl oz) Botran Reserva Blanca
0.75 cl (0.25 fl oz) corn syrup and
Picamas sauce
1.5 cl (0.5 fl oz) Vermouth all'Aceto
Balsamico di Modena PGI Tomaso Agnini

Method: shake
Glass: Cocktail coupe
Garnish: rim with unsweetened cocoa powder

Preparation

Put all of the ingredients in a shaker, stir
and shake with ice. Pour into a cocktail
coupe previously rimmed with unsweetened cocoa powder and cooled.

Nahuatl

Papillon

Ingredients

2.5 cl (0.85 fl oz) Trois Rivières Cuvée de l'Océan
1.5 cl (0.5 fl oz) peach and passion fruit purée
Top-up: Prosecco

Method: shake • Glass: Flute
Garnish: edible flower

Preparation

Put all of the ingredients, except for the Prosecco,
in a shaker, stir and shake with ice. Pour into
a flute, top-up with Prosecco and garnish
with an edible flower.

Port Royal

Ingredients

1.5 cl (0.5 fl oz) Worthy Park Rum-Bar
White Overproof
3 cl (1 fl oz) Madras
3 cl (1 fl oz) Brugal Blanco
1 cl (0.3 fl oz) stout beer syrup
1 cl (0.3 fl oz) Varnelli Moca coffee liqueur
2 dashes Bob's ginger bitters

Method: shake • Glass: Tumbler
Garnish: fresh thyme and cinnamon

Preparation

Put all of the ingredients in a shaker, stir and shake with ice. Pour into a tumbler glass filled with ice cubes. Garnish with a sprig of thyme and a cinnamon stick.

Wari Wari

Ingredients

5 cl (1.7 fl oz) Zafra Master Reserve 21 Años
Muscovado sugar cube
1 dash Spanish Bitters
Lemon peel

Method: build with ice cubes • Glass: Old fashioned
Garnish: rim with sugar and cinammon,
dehydrated orange

Preparation

Soak the sugar cube in Spanish Bitters and dissolve in a tiny amount of water, directly in an old fashioned glass previously rimmed with sugar and cinammon. Add the other ingredients and stir. Stir the drink and add one ice; squeeze lemon zest over the top to release the essential oils into the drink.

Biographies

Giovanna Moldenhauer has been a professional journalist for more than twenty years. As a sommelier, she studies spirits with curiosity and passion, especially rum. She deepens her knowledge by attending festivals, events and previews. Her presentations of various types of distillates, accompanied by unusual combinations proposed by starred chefs, have given rise to articles for established sector-specific publications.

Fabio Petroni studied photography and then collaborated with the most talented professionals in the industry. His line of work led him to specialize in portraits and still life, areas in which he has shown an intuitive and rigorous style. He works with major advertising agencies and has participated in numerous campaigns for prestigious companies known worldwide, including major Italian brands.

Fabio Bacchi, a noted figure in the world of Italian bartending, has mastered his profession over thirty years working for international luxury hotel brands.

Acknowledgements

We would like to thank Giorgio Cotti, Fiorenzo Detti, Linda Nozza and Pietro Pellegrini for sharing their knowledge of the world of rum and helping in the selection of the brands; Italesse for the Wormwood collection (based on the design by Giancarlo Mancino and designer Luca Trezzi) with the Astoria, Alto-Ball, Galante and Fizz models used in the photographs of the cocktails.

Our thanks to the bartending team at The Spirit Milano, one of the top bars in the Milanese and Italian cocktail scene, for the conception, development and creation of the recipes in this book. The team is composed of Carlo Simbula, Vincenzo Losappio, Alessandro Impagnatiello and Bar Manager Fabio Bacchi.

Our thanks to the following companies:
Bolis for Zafra, Compagnia dei Caraibi, D&C SPA, Distilleria Bonaventura Maschio for Botran, Fratelli Branca Distillerie for Mount Gay, Ghilardi Selezioni, Meregalli Vino è Arte for St. Lucia, Onesti Group, Pallini SPA, Pellegrini SPA, Primalux Spirits, Rinaldi Importatori SPA, Rossi & Rossi for Ron Millonario, Savio Trading for Malteco, Velier,

and their representatives:
Andrea Bolis and Massimo Melis, Margherita Vaschetto, Edelberto Baracco, Daniele Bonnin and Fabio Torretta, Marco Sarfatti, Francesco Zara, Pietro Ghilardi and Marianna Sicheri Mazzoleni, Enrico Magnani, Pasquale Damiano, Pietro Pellegrini, Giorgio Paris, Fabrizio Tacchi and Gabriele Rondani, Walter Rossi, Marco Savio, Daniele Biondi who made realizing this publication much easier.

Useful websites

Abuelo Ron 7 Años: www.ronabuelopanama.com

Admiral Rodney St. Lucia Rum: www.saintluciarums.com

Angostura 1919: www.angostura.com

Arcane Extraroma 12 Years Old: www.arcanerum.com

Barbancourt Réserve Spéciale 8 Ans: www.barbancourt.net

Bielle Vieux 2009: www.rhumbielle.com

Botran Reserva Blanca: www.botranrums.com

Brugal Extra Viejo: www.brugal-rum.com

Centenario Gran Legado 12 Años: www.roncentenario.eu

Cihuatán Solera 12 Reserva Especial: www.cihuatanrum.com

Clairin Casimir 3.1: www.thespiritofhaiti.com – www.velier.it

Damoiseau Blanc 40: www.damoiseaurhum.com

Diplomático Reserva Exclusiva: www.rondiplomatico.com

Domaine de Séverin XO: www.severinrhum.com

Don Q Añejo: www.donq.com

Doorly's XO: Facebook Foursquare Rum Distillery

El Dorado 8 Years Old: www.theeldoradorum.com

Flor de Caña Gran Reserva 7 Years Old: www.flordecana.com

Gosling's Black Seal 80 Proof: www.goslingsrum.com

Hampden Fire Velvet Overproof: www.hampdenrumcompany.com

La Hechicera Fine Aged Rum: www.lahechicera.co

Malteco Reserva del Fundador 20 Años: www.saviotrading.it

Mount Gay Black Barrel: www.mountgayrum.com

Neisson Blanc: www.neisson.fr

Père Labat 59: Facebook Distillerie du Père Labat

Plantation 20th Anniversary: www.plantationrum.com

Presidente Marti 15 Años Solera: www.oliveryoliver.com

Reimonenq Cuvée Spéciale Blanc Centenaire: www.musee-du-rhum.fr

Rhum Rhum Blanc PMG: www.velier.it – www.capovilladistillati.it

Roble Viejo Extra Añejo: www.ronroble.com

Ron Millonario Reserva Especial 15 Años: www.ronmillonario.com

Ryoma Rhum Japonais Vieilli 7 Ans: www.primaluxspirits.it

Saint Aubin Premium White Rum: www.rhumsaintaubin.com

Saint James Vieux: www.saintjames-rum.com

Santiago de Cuba Carta Blanca: www.rumsantiago.it

Savanna Grand Arôme Lontan Blanc: www.distilleriesavanna.com

Sol Tarasco Extra Aged: www.charandauruapan.com.mx

Trois Rivières Cuvée de l'Océan: www.plantationtroisrivieres.com

Vanilla Dzama Vieux 10 Years: www.dzama.mg

Worthy Park Rum-Bar White Overproof: www.worthyparkestate.com

Zafra Master Reserve 21 Años: www.zafrarum.com

Photo credits

Project editors
VALERIA MANFERTO DE FABIANIS
LAURA ACCOMAZZO

Graphic design
MARIA CUCCHI

WS White Star Publishers® is a registered trademark
property of White Star s.r.l.

© 2018 White Star s.r.l.
Piazzale Luigi Cadorna, 6 - 20123 Milan, Italy
www.whitestar.it

Translation and Editing: TperTradurre s.r.l.

ISBN 978-88-544-1240-8
1 2 3 4 5 6   22 21 20 19 18

Printed in Cina